The Canadian Parents' Sourcebook:

Everything You Need To Know About Baby Goods and Services

Revised and Updated

Ellen Roseman & Colleen Darragh

Doubleday Canada Limited, Toronto

Interior design by Irene Carefoot
Jacket design by Dragon's Eye Press
Typesetting by Compeer Typographic Services Limited
Printed and bound in Canada by Gagne Printing

Canadian Cataloguing in Publication Data

Roseman, Ellen, 1947–
  The Canadian parents' sourcebook

Rev. ed.
Includes index.
ISBN 0-385-25190-4

1. Infants' supplies — Canada.   2. Consumer
education — Canada.   I. Darragh, Colleen.
II. Title.

RJ61.R68 1989   649'.122   C88-095415-9

Published in Canada by
  Doubleday Canada Limited
  105 Bond Street
  Toronto, Ontario
  M5B 1Y3

Contents

For Edward, Charles and Richard (E.R.)

For my parents (C.D.)

Acknowledgements

We would like to offer a special thanks to the many people who contributed their time, their experience and their advice to this book. Whether they were parents or child-care professionals, their help was expert and eager. We appreciate their generosity.

Among them: Anna Barron, Sharon Darragh, Eve Drobot, Dr. Heather Foster, Martha Friendly, Batya Hebdon, Joy Jacoby, Doug Johnson, Chris Kennedy, Anne Leekam, Dr. Anne Marriott, Evelyne McDonald, Boyd Neil, Irene Pojaujis, Cathy Scott, Stephen Sher, and Monica Voss. Thanks also to Nancy Colbert and Geoffrey Stevens.

Our editors, Denise Schon and Shauna Sanders, deserve a word of gratitude too. Their editorial skills, coupled with their personal enthusiasm for the project, made the publication of *The Canadian Parents' Sourcebook* a family affair.

Girls and boys have been given equal time throughout this book, to avoid sexism. "He" and "she" are used in alternating chapters.

Introduction

When the first edition of *The Canadian Parents' Sourcebook* appeared in bookstores over two years ago, we hoped that it would find a comfortable corner for itself on shelves that were spilling over with parenting guides of every description.

But much to our amazement — and delight — the *Sourcebook* did much more than that. It quickly became a Canadian bestseller, and its popularity continues to grow. Parents across the country have told us how much they relied on the book as they shopped for baby equipment, searched for child care and prepared the house for the arrival of a new baby.

The *Sourcebook* is still the only guide of its kind in Canada. Because the baby-care scene changes so rapidly, however (with new products, new ideas, new safety concerns), we decided that it was time to revise it. This edition reflects the most up-to-date information available on buying for the Canadian baby.

Although we have thoroughly researched the items included in this book, it should be noted that it is virtually impossible to guarantee that the prices you find when you go shopping will always match the ones listed here. Prices are subject to change, and will vary according to increases in manufacturing costs. You will also notice that prices will differ, sometimes slightly, sometimes substantially, in your local retail outlets. We recommend that you shop around for the best price, without overlooking the value of expert advice and follow-up service.

Similarly, experience has taught us that the baby-care industry is a volatile one, and companies and products can vanish quickly. So while we are confident that the names and items that appear here are currently accurate, some may disappear tomorrow — only to be replaced by a fresh crop of enthusiastic inventors.

One of the pleasures we have enjoyed since the publication of *The Canadian Parents' Sourcebook* is the response from readers. Our conversations with parents have helped us to make improvements to this newest edition.

We welcome your contribution, too. You can play a part in future editions of this book. Contact us if you have suggestions, if you want to tell us about your own parenting experiences — even if you want to point out our mistakes! You can reach us by sending your comments to Doubleday Canada Limited, 105 Bond Street, Toronto, Ontario M5B 1Y3.

In the meantime, we hope that this book helps you to make the right choices for you and your child.

Colleen Darragh
Ellen Roseman
January, 1989

CHAPTER 1

Starting Out

YOU CAN SPEND thousands of dollars on your baby, or you can spend next to nothing. It all depends on your budget, your taste, and the generosity of your friends and relatives. Few parents know ahead of time exactly how much it will cost to outfit the new child.

What *is* certain is that there has never been such a terrific choice in baby paraphernalia. There is a mini-baby boom in Canada and the baby industry has grown along with it. Stores are filled with furniture, toys, accessories, and clothing catering to the new parent. Some of this merchandise is essential; a lot of it is utterly useless.

If you find the selection overwhelming, you're not alone. Parents are often hesitant to spend money on baby gear they may not need. They are swamped by products and advertising claims, when what they need is solid information.

To avoid being besieged when you shop, take the same approach to buying for the baby that you take when you buy for yourself. Use a consumer's perspective. Do your homework. Read up on products before you arrive in the store. Comparison-shop. Insist on value for your dollar.

Find out which manufacturers' products are the best quality. Study the top-of-the-line items (even if you can't afford them) to see what they offer and what features are important to you. In cribs, the top name is Little Folks; in strollers, Perego; in high chairs, Fisher-Price; in car seats, Cosco; in baby carriers, Baby Matey.

Don't assume that a good manufacturer in one category is automatically good in another. Fisher-Price makes great high chairs, but their changing table is considered over-priced by many parents and their car seat failed to meet Canadian standards and never made it to the market. Reputations must be earned on each product individually.

Inevitably you will fall in love with an item or two (baby things are supposed to be lovable, after all) and common sense will fly out the window. All parents can ruefully rhyme off a few mistakes they've made. But when you make an effort to find out what's available, what's essential and what's not, your impulse buys will be fewer. And the choices you make will be good ones.

Many couples are nervous about furnishing the nursery ahead of time. Preoccupied with the baby's safe passage through childbirth, they worry that their beautiful furniture may have to be dismantled and returned.

However, this procrastination has a price. The first few weeks after the baby comes home are a hectic, tiring time. As you cope with 24-hour demand feedings, unexpected visitors, and the challenge of caring for a newborn, the last thing you need is to be running around doing errands. As one experienced mother says, "It's easier to look after the baby when he's on the inside."

If you simply can't bring yourself to pre-furnish the nursery, you can shop ahead at stores that will hold your purchases until after the baby is born. Just make sure you measure the baby's room first, to see if everything fits, and ask the store for help in setting up the items. Most baby furniture today comes in pieces and you have to assemble it yourself. With a new baby on your hands, you probably won't have the time or energy to follow complicated directions for putting your crib or changing table together.

The long months of pregnancy are also a good time to send for mail order catalogues and browse through them. You can find many unusual items in these catalogues that you won't spot in stores, but keep in mind that delivery takes at least four to six weeks and that not all items meet Canadian safety standards. And if the items don't live up to their billing — a common problem with mail order shopping — you need time to return them and get your money back.

Planning your needs and purchases in advance will also help you avoid duplication. If friends or relatives ask for suggestions on baby gifts, be honest. Let them know what you need and don't need. Or you can register your preferences with a store, just as a bride and groom do, and refer friends and relatives there.

WHERE TO BUY

There are several sources of baby equipment. Our choice for first-time parents is a good specialty store, a shop run by experienced parents who know what they're selling and give helpful advice. Prices may be higher at baby boutiques than at the discount chains, but it's worth paying a little extra for service. Look for a store that will help you assemble your baby furniture and will take it back without question if you have a problem.

Discount chains such as Consumers Distributing, Toy City, and Toys 'R' Us offer great prices on baby goods, but they're not known for after-sale service. We recommend them for items that are low in price and unlikely to break down. If you know exactly what you want and how to use it, the discounters may be right for you. But if you need an informed opinion about what to buy, don't expect them to provide it.

Department stores carry baby equipment and are usually

reliable for follow-up service. They also have regular sales.

Comparison-shop so you get the best value. Don't overlook the large home furnishing stores as sources of baby gear. Ikea, for example, carries a line of affordable infant furniture like cribs, changing tables, and high chairs, all styled with Scandinavian simplicity.

THE BABY BUDGET

On some baby items, it makes sense to be stingy. On others, it's advisable to buy the best quality you can afford. When should you splurge and when should you economize? Your yardstick should be safety and the length of time you will need each item.

If you buy a poorly made crib, you'll probably have to replace it. Chances are you'll buy a more expensive crib the second time around, and wind up paying more than if you had bought quality furniture in the first place. A well-made crib can be passed on to the next child, or sold later at a good price if you no longer need it.

If you must scrimp, scrimp on smaller pieces with a short life span. An infant seat is used for only a few months and doesn't have to be made of extremely high-quality materials. Find a low-priced infant seat and spend your money on a good high chair or stroller — items that will receive daily use for several years.

Secondhand stores and garage sales are a godsend for some new parents. Very few of us can immediately afford to buy everything we want for the baby. But if we can pick up slightly used items at half the cost of new, our budgets can stretch a lot further.

You may be able to find many gently-used baby items at secondhand stores or garage sales. Remember, however, that older cribs, car seats, and playpens may not meet current safety regulations. It's up to you to assure yourself of every article's safety. Check with your local office of Consumer and

Corporate Affairs Canada. It's also important to find out if all the necessary pieces are included, if you can buy more, and if there are any instructions for use.

Browsing through secondhand stores is a good way to check on the quality of baby furniture. Even if you don't intend to buy a used item, you can investigate how well a new model will withstand abuse. If you spot a nearly-new model that looks as if it's been torture-tested, don't buy it, new or old.

Borrowing baby items from friends and relatives costs even less, but the same warnings about safety and missing parts apply. Don't assume that anything is acceptable before you check it out. It's better to borrow items that are used for only a short time, rather than buy them, since the more you buy, the more you'll have to store later on.

Borrowing is also a good way to run your own performance tests. After a week's use, you should be able to judge whether an item works for your child. Some babies love automatic swings, for example, while others are terrified of them. Trying out a product first helps you avoid an unnecessary purchase. And if you do decide to buy one, a trial run will help you decide which features you like.

Another way to save money is to buy combination pieces, items that have several uses around the house. A changing table, when the baby outgrows it, can double as a planter, a TV stand, or a toy shelf. A high chair can be used as a play desk. Manufacturers often design their furniture with convertibility in mind. But make sure the item really performs all its intended functions. If it does none of them very well, you're better off buying a functional single-use piece and selling it later.

Avoid buying a lot of clothes, bedding and toys before the baby is born, particularly stretch sleepers, sweater sets, stuffed animals, and blankets. Wait to see how many you receive as gifts and then fill in the gaps. Buying clothes for babies is risky because they grow so fast. They're never in one size for very long.

Waiting until after the baby is born makes sense for other items as well. You don't know what kind of infant you have until you get acquainted with each other. Depending on the baby's temperament, you may not need certain things you had considered essential. Babies are surprising creatures. If your baby has long fussy periods and needs constant cuddling, you may never use the portable crib you were given. A baby carrier such as a Snugli may be in constant use, since many fretful babies are calmed when they are zipped into a frontpack. Yet some babies, strangely enough, love to sleep in a portable crib and scream blue murder when carried around in a Snugli. You never know what will work until you try it.

Be sure to buy the essential items in advance. Once you have them, you should set them up and try to figure out how to use them. Struggling with a complex stroller while your baby is screaming is not a happy experience on your first outing together; learning how to strap him in the car seat the same day you take him home from the hospital is even more frustrating. Last-minute fumbling, when you are nervous as only a new parent can be, can mean disaster.

Using baby equipment properly takes practice and it's easier to get the hang of it without a real live (often crying) baby to contend with. Practise with a life-sized doll, or, using a giant leap of imagination, try a 10-pound sack of potatoes. Make an effort to master the technique before you try it on your new infant. Not only is your convenience at stake, but your child's safety as well.

When you try out the equipment, check to see if everything works as it should. Are all the parts included? Are there any sharp edges or extrusions, any exposed screws or bolts? Is the instruction booklet clear and easy to follow? If anything is amiss, follow it up *now* when you have the time. Later, you may be too busy.

In the last few months of pregnancy, you should also start preparing the baby's room. Buy the crib (or at least order it), along with the other essentials: a dresser, changing table, rocking chair, and lamp. And don't forget the colourful wallpaper, wall hangings or murals. Babies need visual stimulation as well as creature comforts.

With the nursery equipped and decorated, you will be able to welcome the baby home in style. Best of all, you will be free to devote your time and energies to what really counts — getting to know and love your new family member.

Another point to consider when you're buying baby gear is that you could budget for babysitting expenses instead of splurging on a luxury item for the baby. For example, passing up the deluxe playpen could leave you with enough money to hire a babysitter for five or six Saturday nights. Be good to yourself, not just the baby, so that your first year together is as relaxed as you can make it.

MAIL ORDER CATALOGUES

The biggest and best baby catalogue comes from Mothercare, a British retail chain. More than 200 pages long and mailed anywhere in the world, this catalogue carries everything from maternity clothes to prams to layette woollies. Mothercare customers swear by the quality of the workmanship. For a copy, write to Mothercare-by-Post, P.O. Box 145, Watford, England.

A Canadian catalogue worth checking out is Baby Love Products, published by Grace Marcinkoski in Alberta. It contains sixty-eight pages of useful baby items, including sewing patterns for infant wardrobes and one-size-fits-all cotton diapers with Velcro closures. She also carries replacement parts for many baby items. For a copy, write to 5015–46 Street, Camrose, Alberta, T4V 3G3.

Born to Love is a collection of hard-to-find products. Publisher Cathy McDiarmid also produces Canadian Family Resources, a booklet listing more than 600 Canadian

Mail Order Catalogues, cont'd:

magazines, newsletters, and mail order suppliers for families. Updated twice a year, it's $3.75 a copy, or $14 for a two-year subscription. You can reach her at 21 Potsdam Rd., Unit 61, Downsview, Ontario, M3N 1N3.

If your local bookstore doesn't carry a selection of baby books, you can order from Parentbooks, 201 Harbord St., Toronto, Ontario M5S 1H6. Ask for the titles you want, or name a specific subject and the owners will put together a short reading list for you.

The Sheepskin Company catalogue includes lambskin comforters, bunting bags, car seat covers, toys, and hats. Write to them at 86-07 Eliot Avenue, Rego Park, New York 11374. The catalogue costs $1 U.S.

Babies by Storm sells frontpacks and backpacks, diaper bags, and patterns. Write to them at Box 1623, Springfield, Ohio 45501.

Whole Life is another catalogue with books on birth and parenting, as well as soothing music on tapes. The emphasis in this catalogue is on holistic health, herbs, and expanded consciousness. For a copy, send $2 to Whole Life, RR2, Powassan, Ontario, P0H 1Z0.

Childworks by Family Bazaar offers nursery accessories, unique toys, clothes, and infant furnishings. Write to them at 352 Evelyn Street, Paramus, New Jersey 07652.

U-Bild sells patterns for juvenile furniture and play equipment, for the do-it-yourselfer. Write to them at Box 2383, Van Nuys, California 91409.

BIGGEST MISTAKES

Here's a list of a few of the products some parents regretted buying or borrowing:

- "A pram. We only used it two or three times. It was heavy to lift up and down stairs and we could only use it to walk around the neighbourhood. It's an item parents seem to buy for themselves, not the baby."

- "A futon mattress. I had it custom-made and it turned out to be the wrong size for the crib. It's also not machine washable."

- "A bath sling. It was only about $5 but it was useless."

- "A playpen. The baby never sat in it and it took up a lot of space."

- "A high chair. We fed the baby in her infant chair and later she preferred the clip-on chair that lets her sit with us at the table."

CHAPTER 2

The Nursery

FOR THE NEXT YEAR or two the nursery will be the most important room in your house. Making it comfortable and inviting can be a delightful introduction to parenting.

Try to provide a stimulating environment for the baby from the moment you arrive home from the hospital. Although babies are not able to see colour for four or five months, studies indicate that objects with patterns in bright or highly contrasting colours catch and hold their interest. (Black-and-white mobiles capture baby's attention.) Concentrate on visual appeal in the crib accessories, the wall hangings, even on the ceiling.

Let your imagination loose. One nursery decorator suggests bringing the sky right into the nursery by covering the ceiling in pastel blue, then with white semi-gloss latex, painting on a handful of fluffy clouds. Or add charm and contrast with wallpaper, pictures, and bright flooring.

A baby's nursery can take on any look you want to create, from country-style to classic to contemporary. But let practicality guide you, too. Make this an easy-care room, one that can handle baby activity with ease. Scrubbable surfaces, machine-washable fabrics, and a convenient furniture layout are essential.

Studies show that lack of stimulation can make a baby cranky and bored. But does a parent have to worry about overdoing it? Apparently not. Babies have an innate reflex that copes with overstimulation. Faced with too many people, sounds or bright colours, babies simply shut their eyes and go to sleep.

CRADLES AND BASSINETS

Your baby's first bed should be a warm and snug one. That means the crib will probably lie empty for a little while.

Somehow a crib doesn't seem right for a tiny baby. Cribs are so large they tend to swallow up a newborn. The small space of a cradle or a bassinet is far more intimate and cosy. It also allows you to move the baby easily from room to room. You may prefer to keep the baby at your bedside at night so she's close at hand for feeding or nursing and so you can check on her. Then during the day you can carry or roll her bed into the nursery for her naps.

Bassinets are small wicker beds on wheels; cradles are wooden beds that rock with a touch of your hand or foot. Swinging or "pendulum" cradles can be removed from their stands.

If you're offered a cradle or bassinet on loan, you're in luck. (If not, ask your relatives to search their attics. One mother discovered a family heirloom that way: a handsome Quebec pine cradle that had been forgotten for years.) You can also look for secondhand versions. Some couples scour flea markets or country auctions to find one-of-a-kind nursery items like this. But stay away from cradles made before 1974, because they did not have to meet any safety regulations.

Stores specializing in handcrafted pine and oak furniture often carry antique reproductions of cradles. Jolly Jumper makes several models of cradles.

Buying one for $90 or $100 or up may not be worthwhile, however. The problem with cradles and bassinets is that babies outgrow them so quickly. After three months, they start to feel confined in them. And once they begin rolling from side to side and pulling themselves up (at three to five months), they're no longer safe in such a small bed. Instead of buying a cradle, you might consider renting one from a local baby store. A reasonable rental fee is $20 or $30 for three months.

Crib Cuddle, a hammocklike sleeping unit that fits inside a crib, was a gimmicky product, expensive ($40 and up), and came with a heartbeat sound mechanism to make the infant feel right at home. But the product safety branch of Consumer and Corporate Affairs Canada issued a warning about the possible dangers of the Crib Cuddle when improperly installed. With all the bad publicity, sales died right off. The item is now discontinued.

If you don't want to buy, use your ingenuity. Your carriage can double as a bed. Or you can fashion a simple wicker laundry basket into a baby cot by decorating it with nursery linens.

There are safety standards for cradles, as there are for cribs. They were passed in 1974, and any cradles made before then may be unsafe. Under the safety rules, all cradles must have no more than 6 centimetres (or $2^3/8$ inches) of space between the upright bars or slats. And any device used to rock the cradle must not allow it to swing very far.

Your best choice is a cradle that can be locked into a non-rocking position. Babies don't like to rock all the time, especially if their own movements cause the rocking. With an older cradle, you may have to prop a book underneath one rocker to keep it still.

If you choose a swinging cradle, be sure the stand is sturdy and has a wide base.

Cradles can't be folded or packed away easily after the baby stops using them, an important consideration for parents living in apartments or those planning to move frequently. But they do have a good resale value and can be used for other purposes. Once outgrown, a cradle can serve as a container for firewood, plants, magazines, or toys.

Unlike cradles, bassinets have no specific safety standards. Check wicker bassinets for loose webbing that might poke the baby. The bassinet may come with a mattress (generally, a thin foam pad covered with vinyl). If not, you can cut a piece of foam to fit, or buy a ready-made mattress, but make sure the mattress fits snugly so the baby's face cannot be caught between the side of the mattress and the bed.

If you decorate with ruffles, skirts, and pads, don't use any padding that will raise the baby dangerously high. When lining the basket, be sure the material can't slide down to cover the baby's face. And forget about pillows—the baby doesn't need one and there's a slight risk of smothering. Bassinet bedding can be custom-made at linen specialty shops, so if you have a bassinet frame but you can't sew a stitch, you can still make it beautiful.

TRAVEL BEDS AND BASKETS

A travel bed or a "Moses basket" (a straw or bullrush basket with handles) can be handy for the baby's first few months, inside the house and out. You can use it as a bed when you go visiting or you can put the baby to sleep in one at home and keep her nearby.

Sharon, 28, finds that a baby basket is a terrific daytime bed for her newborn daughter Shannon. "When she was upstairs in her bedroom I worried about not being able to hear her. So I keep her near me in the family room in her basket. I can check on her from the kitchen, which adjoins the family room, and the activity around the house doesn't seem to disturb her sleep at all. If I want to move her back to her bedroom, I don't have to wake her up."

You can buy a handwoven baby basket, with a canopy, ruffles, and bedding included, at prices ranging from $60 to $275. Holt Renfrew sells the *haute couture* model, lined with designer linens. At the lower end of the price scale, the baskets are still charming. A stand for a baby basket, with two wheels for easy moving, costs about $40. The stand can also be used for a baby bath, and later for a laundry basket.

Snugli makes a "carry" bed, a portable bed with mesh sides and a padded-foam bottom. The bed zips down to store flat and has sturdy carrying straps.

Also available are fabric carry baskets, such as Bo Peep's Travel Tender and Formelco's Karry Kot, or foam travel cribs. Like all such portable cribs, these are designed for mobility. If you use a portable crib as a substitute for a bassinet or crib, keep in mind that it is not as sturdily constructed.

CHOOSING A CRIB

A crib is more than a piece of furniture. It's the only place in your home where you leave a child alone for long periods of time. So it's vital that the crib you choose provides a safe environment for your baby. Luckily, today's cribs combine both contemporary design and safety features.

If you're buying a brand-new crib, your budget is the primary consideration. New cribs start at about $150 and rise to $700 in price. Cribs are generally sold without a mattress, so remember to budget an extra $50 to $100 for one. (More about crib mattresses later in this chapter.)

Avoid the lowest-priced models if you plan to have more than one child. They aren't built to last, though they are safe. All new cribs must meet federal safety standards.

The lowest-priced cribs are made by Stork Craft, a company in Richmond, British Columbia, which sells more cribs than any other manufacturer. Kid Kraft, a division of Dorel Ltd. in Montreal, makes a medium-priced crib line. Higher-priced cribs are made by Lepine, Morigeau, Young Generation, Torpedo, Benjamin and Little Folks. Stork Craft cribs, despite their low price, are "safe and solid, easy to put together and easy to maintain," said *Canadian Consumer* magazine in a test report published in April, 1988. It rated a $130 Stork Craft crib the best buy among a group of ten going up to $580 in price.

Medium and higher-priced cribs have more curves than straight lines. (The more curves, the more expensive the crib.) They have sturdier corner posts, finer sanding and detailing, and more unusual endboard designs. The screws fit inside threaded sleeves, so the wood won't be stripped or the holes become too large. There is often a steel stabilizing bar underneath the springs for added support. And you will pay more, of course, for modern design or a traditional look. If it's a fashionable crib, the price tag is higher.

The crib you select should have several mattress positions so you can lower the mattress as the baby grows. Most cribs have at least one side that drops down, giving you easy access to the baby. More expensive cribs have double drop sides, allowing you to put the crib anywhere in the room and to remove the baby from either side. (Single drop sides, however, *are* more stable.)

Check for wheels or casters, which allow you to move the crib away from the wall to change sheets or to vacuum. (If your child bounces and jumps a lot in the crib, the casters can always be removed.) And look for "teething rails," plastic strips that protect the side rails from teeth marks and the baby from splinters. Metal cribs do not need them.

Cribs usually have metal springs to support the mattress, but those made by Stork Craft have wooden floorboards. There are no studies proving which type of support is better, but both kinds can accommodate a foam mattress. (Some people prefer the foam mattress, which is lighter and less expensive.)

If your child's room is small and space is at a premium, look for a crib with built-in drawers underneath. The area below the crib is wasted space, which can be better used for storage. The drawers also add stability to the crib. You may also want to consider a crib that converts to a youth bed. Once a child is 89 centimetres (or 35 inches) tall, it's time to move her out of a crib. A youth bed is halfway between a crib and a regular-sized bed. After your child has outgrown the crib, you can remove one side and use it as a day bed or loveseat if there is enough room in the nursery. This can be a special place to read stories together, or a unique play area.

Safety comes first, but consider style too. It may be worthwhile to you to pay extra for a distinctive-looking crib, since it will be part of the nursery decor for a few years. And there is a wide choice of cribs that have attractive designs and reasonable price tags.

But don't forget the baby's point of view. Some crib styles are designed to please adults' tastes, not infants'.

CRIBS AND SAFETY

Safety standards for cribs were established in October, 1973, and updated in September, 1986. They were designed to prevent serious accidents such as strangulation, suffocation, and falls. Any crib made since 1974 carries the date of manufacture, model number, and name and address of the manufacturer or importer. If you're buying a secondhand crib, look for this information. If it is not there, you will have to modify the crib to meet current safety standards. Don't buy a secondhand crib made before 1981. There are just too many potential hazards.

However, modifying a secondhand crib or even buying a brand-new one is no guarantee of your baby's safety. You still have to be vigilant about maintaining it.

All cribs should be assembled strictly according to the manufacturer's instructions. If the instructions are missing, ask the retailer or manufacturer for a spare copy (and ask for help if you can't decipher them). Keep the instructions close at hand for reference, and if you pass the crib along to a relative or friend, be sure to include them.

Examine your crib from time to time, whether it's new or secondhand. Sharp edges, corners, and protruding nuts can cause a baby serious injury. Babies can also swallow or bite into parts that have broken off. If the teething rail begins to crack, replace it immediately. Splinters of plastic from broken rails could harm your child.

It's especially important to check the crib once your child begins to pull herself up, stand, bounce, and jump. Shake the crib from time to time to be sure the bolts or other hardware parts are still firmly attached.

A potential hazard arises from the Gate-A-Way crib, made by Dorel of Montreal. The crib has a side rail that can be lowered to a horizontal position under the mattress. Consumer and Corporate Affairs put out a warning in June, 1988, that parents should never leave a baby unattended with the crib side under the mattress in case of falls.

The mattress support system of any crib should also be carefully watched. Almost every crib sold in Canada until fall, 1986, was made the same way: a mattress support board is attached to the frame with four S-shaped hooks. Accidents can occur when the S-shaped hook attached to the mattress platform becomes dislodged in one corner. This can happen when the sheets are changed, or when another child (or large dog) plays under the crib. It can happen when a child jumps on the mattress. Even a sudden jolt to the crib can dislodge the hangers.

This is a potentially fatal hazard. If one corner of the support system becomes detached, the mattress tends to tilt downwards in that corner. The danger is that the child can slip between the mattress and the frame — and suffocate.

Any crib with a suspended mattress support system is vulnerable to this hazard, but publicity centred around Stork Craft Ltd., Canada's largest crib manufacturer. A number of babies died in older Stork Craft cribs, models made before March, 1982, when the company introduced a locking device.

Other manufacturers have followed Stork Craft's lead and introduced locking devices for their cribs. If you can't find a locking device for your brand of crib, you can support the mattress with a long low table or several cartons full of books. Then, if a hanger accidentally dislodges in one corner, the mattress won't sag or tilt downwards.

Following inquests into the deaths of several babies in Stork Craft cribs without hanger-locking plugs, the company announced a national crib registration program starting in 1985. Its toll-free number for crib registration is 1-800-663-5003.

Once your name and address are on file with the manufacturer, you can be notified about developing safety problems and the availability of safety devices, such as hanger-locking plugs. If you find a registration form included with your new crib, fill it out and send it back. This is very important. (If you buy or inherit an older crib, you should contact the manufacturer too. If there is any new safety information to be passed on, you'll want to hear about it.)

In September, 1986, new federal standards for mattress supports came into effect. Manufacturers *have* eliminated the S-shaped hooks and locking plugs and are generally bolting the mattress support board into the crib frame. This makes changing the mattress position more difficult but most parents find that only two positions are needed — a higher one for infants and a lower one for older babies.

Cribs made before September, 1986, are no longer allowed to be sold in secondhand stores, but you may still find one at a garage sale or inherit one from a friend or relative. If so, be sure to ask the manufacturer or a local baby store for locking hardware (about $35). This will make it almost as safe as a new crib. Don't use it unless it can be updated.

In 1989, the rules were to be changed again to reduce the risks from horizontal bars and openings on crib panels, which babies can use as a toehold to climb out. Manufacturers have already agreed voluntarily to revise their designs.

CRIB SAFETY CHECKLIST

When buying a crib, either new or used, or when refurbishing an old crib for your new baby, check for the following safety features:

- There should be no more than 6 centimetres (2^3/$_8$ inches) between the bars or slats. Cribs with wider openings might permit a child to squeeze through feet first.

- There should be a double lock on the drop side so it cannot be operated by the baby in the crib or by a child playing outside the crib.

- With the mattress support board in its lowest position, measure the distance between it and the top of the sides. This distance should be at least 66 centimetres (26 inches) to prevent the baby from falling out of the crib. The top of the drop side, when lowered, should remain at least 23 centimetres (9 inches) above the mattress support board when it is adjusted to its higher position.

- Push the mattress into one corner. There should be a gap of no more than 3.8 centimetres (1½ inches) between the mattress and the opposite side of the crib frame to prevent suffocation. Also, the mattress should not be any thicker than 15 centimetres (6 inches).

- Avoid cribs that have corner posts any higher than 3 millimetres (1/8 inch). Otherwise, a baby's clothing could become caught up on them and cause the child to strangle. Cut-out designs in end panels or headboards can be extremely dangerous. Cover them up.

- The end panels on cribs should always extend well below the mattress support. If they don't, your baby's head, arms or legs could become trapped in the space between

---

Crib Safety Checklist, cont'd:

the mattress support and the bottom of the panel. To prevent this from happening, use pegboard to fill the gap.

• Cribs with move-away sides, such as the Gate-A-Way, should have extra locking mechanisms that can only be activated by an adult. They should also have a warning label about the potential hazard of leaving a child unattended unless the side is in the normal use position.

CRIB MATTRESSES

Even if you economize on a crib, you shouldn't scrimp on a mattress. Your child will be sleeping on this surface at least twelve hours a day, soiling it, spilling things on it, standing up and sitting down on it, bouncing and jumping on it, using it as a trampoline and a launching pad for out-of-crib expeditions. You need a mattress that can withstand a lot of abuse.

Crib mattresses start at about $30 and go up to $100 or more. The medium-priced crib mattresses are made by Totkins. Manufacturers of medium and higher-priced crib mattresses are Kantwet, Bo Peep, Marshall, and Little Folks (all in Ontario), Little Darlings, and Baby Tyme, a division of Dorel in Montreal.

Most people buy a coil innerspring mattress, though urethane foam is growing in popularity. A foam mattress is lighter, easier to lift when changing sheets, and generally costs less than an innerspring mattress ($30 to $70). And foam is non-allergenic, while some coil mattresses contain fibres that can cause sneezing or skin irritation. But coils last much longer, while foam wears out after one child.

Water-filled mattresses, something new in the baby market, should be avoided. Several Canadian infants have died on waterbeds in the last few years. A recent case involved Ontario twins who were placed on a waterbed when their parents took them visiting at a friend's home. When the babies were checked after twenty minutes, they had stopped breathing.

The Canadian Pediatric Society recommends that babies sleep on firm surfaces. It does not advise using infant-sized waterbed crib mattresses. Babies can turn their heads when they are on a firm surface but soft waterbeds make movement like this more difficult for a young infant.

You know it's important to buy a good mattress, but how do you select one? The various types look very much alike and major differences in quality are on the inside where you can't see them. Mattresses, unfortunately, are a blind item.

You will improve your chances of finding a good product if you shop at a recognized store selling nationally-advertised brands. A store like Sears makes it easy for you by offering four qualities of crib mattress — from Sears Best to Economy — and detailing the design of each one. (Sears has recently introduced a musical mattress, with a built-in music box.)

You can also learn a lot by sizing up the warranty. Manufacturers who are confident of the quality of their mattresses will guarantee them for five years or more. If the mattress comes with a short warranty or no warranty at all, you can't expect much in the way of durability.

A good crib mattress, one you can expect to outlast more than your first child, will have a covering made of waterproof heavy-gauge vinyl that does not tear easily. Quilted covers look cute, but have a tendency to split when they are wet. (Since vinyl can be hot and uncomfortable with just a cotton sheet over it, we recommend putting a machine-washable quilted cotton pad or fitted terrycloth crib sheet over the vinyl covering.)

If you buy an innerspring mattress, it's worthwhile to ask about the coil count. Some mattresses have as few as thirty-six coils, others as many as 200. Generally speaking, a good innerspring mattress will have a minimum of 100 coils and ideally 130 or more.

Coil counts can be misleading, however, since they depend

on the type of metal used. Some manufacturers use thinner gauge metal, while others use thicker gauge metal (the same as in adult mattresses). A mattress with a high coil count may be less sturdy than one with fewer, thicker coils.

A good crib mattress will have a thick layer of jute or foam over the coils and under the covering. (Foam acts as an insulator and also as a fire-retardant.) Another measure of quality is the way the coils are interconnected or individually pocketed.

If you choose a foam mattress, remember that the density of the foam will determine the resiliency and firmness. A thick foam mattress is not necessarily better than a thin one. A dense foam core is what counts. You have to rely on the retailer and manufacturer to steer you to the best quality.

Futons, the Japanese-style cotton-filled mattresses sold as beds or couches for adults, now come in crib sizes too. But these are impractical since they are not waterproof or machine-washable, and there is a danger of smothering. If you like futons, you will probably prefer to wait until your child is older before you invest in one for her.

Whether you choose a foam or a coil innerspring mattress, it should fit snugly within the crib. You shouldn't be able to get more than two fingers between the mattress and the crib rails and endboards. A gap between the sides of the bed and the mattress can cause suffocation if a baby rolls inside.

There are no government standards for crib mattress sizes, but a new group is working on voluntary guidelines. The Canadian Juvenile Products Association, which represents the major manufacturers, was formed in 1986 to set standards for baby products not regulated by the federal government. Because of consumer concerns about crib safety, it has made standard mattress dimensions its first priority.

If you have had problems with irregularly-sized mattresses or cribs, the association would appreciate your comments. You can write to CJPA executive director Henry Wittenberg at P.O. Box 294, Kleinburg, Ont. L0J 1C0, or call 416-893-1689.

LINEN

Baby linen gets the same deluxe treatment that grown-up bedding enjoys now. Designer looks are plentiful. There's an assortment of lively colours and whimsical patterns, with no lack of practicality. You can co-ordinate, mix and match, choose bunnies, teddies, or ducks, insist on natural fibres only—and you'll still be able to toss all the baby's bedding into the washing machine.

You can't have enough small linen for a baby. Infants create mounds of laundry and linen is high on the list. Stock up on cot, crib and carriage sheets and receiving blankets. Always keep texture in mind when you shop for bedding for your baby. Stroke it and imagine it next to a baby's soft skin. Natural fibres like cotton, brushed flannel, soft wool, terrycloth, and lambskin are good choices.

Bumper pads are an essential purchase. These are the plump pads that line the sides of the crib. They cushion the crib bars, creating a soft spot for the baby's head to nestle against. By preventing her arms and legs from slipping through the bars, they help her sleep better. They also stop drafts.

You'll pay $30 to $50 for a bumper pad alone, $75 or more for a set which includes a matching quilt, sheet, and pillow. We recommend a fabric bumper pad with an attached "safety sheet." Although the safety sheet may make it harder to change the bed, it avoids any risk of the child getting her arms or legs caught in the bars. It also completes the look because it wraps around the mattress. And fabric bumper pads, unlike vinyl, are softer and there is less chance of them sweating. Vinyl-covered bumpers tend to crack after repeated washings. Fabric-covered pads are more durable and well worth the higher price tag.

When choosing a design, look for something colourful. Avoid plain white, even if it coordinates better with your nursery decor. Bumper pads should be bright and stimulating because the baby's head will most often be turned to the side during the first few months. (This is because of a protective condition called the tonic neck reflex.) As a result, bumper pads are even more visible to the baby than mobiles.

The bumper pad should be attached to the crib in at least six places. Once you have tied it on with strong knots, trim the tails so the baby won't get tangled in them. Check the fastenings regularly to make sure they're secure. A vinyl bumper pad should be removed as soon as the baby is able to stand. Otherwise, it can serve as a steppingstone for climbing out of the crib. Large stuffed toys should be removed from the crib for the same reason. (Fabric bumpers tend to collapse if a child stands on them.) If you don't have a bumper pad, you can devise a temporary substitute by weaving a folded blanket through the crib bars. This is particularly helpful when travelling.

As for bedding, you'll need at least four sheets—bottoms only. Top sheets are impractical since babies sleep best wrapped only in a receiving blanket or comforter. Fitted sheets make bed-changing easier. You may find that stretchy cotton-knit sheets slip more easily onto crib mattresses than the woven percale kind.

You should also plan to buy a couple of waterproof crib sheets (about $10 to $15 each). They're called dry-mat and come in several sizes. These are flannel sheets laminated to a piece of rubber which you put next to the mattress, rubber side down, and cover with a bottom sheet. The flannel provides an extra layer of padding and the rubber prevents moisture from leaking through to the mattress.

Receiving blankets are indispensable. You should have at least five to ten of these pint-size flannelette covers on hand ($10 to $20), not only for swaddling the baby but for wiping up unexpected spills and dribbles. Cloth diapers also come in handy for absorbing spit-ups.

You'll need a fuzzy or quilted blanket for cooler weather. If you choose a traditional fleece blanket, avoid styles with long fringes that could loosen and be swallowed. With quilted blankets or comforters, look closely at the stitching to be sure there are no loops or loose threads to catch on baby's fingers and toes. And check to see that all stuffing is where it belongs, on the inside.

Lambskin comforters are growing increasingly popular. They have been used in New Zealand and Australia for many years as substitutes for crib sheets, with excellent results. "Mothers have found that even distressed and irritable babies sleep longer, settle down more quickly and actually sleep more soundly," says one distributor. And a Cambridge University study has confirmed that lambswool helps impart a feeling of security and well-being. Sometimes a colicky baby is calmed by the lambskin's soft touch on her skin. (Many children use the comforters as security blankets.)

Lambskin mats are machine washable, warm in winter and cool in summer, and safe for babies who sleep face down because they allow continuous air circulation under the baby. They can be used in car seats, high chairs, strollers, playpens, backpacks, carriers—just about anywhere. They're pricey ($50 and up), but worth suggesting as a gift to someone who wants to splurge on you. Snugli makes a lambskin comforter that is machine washable. Sears sells a lambskin, but it must be dry cleaned.

Duvets, or down comforters, are available in crib sizes. These cosy lightweight comforters are ideal for tucking around the baby and keeping her snug. They come with both down and polyester fillings (the polyester fibres are non-allergenic), they are usually machine washable, and you can buy ready-made duvet covers or have them custom-made. Try specialty shops or look in the Mothercare mail order catalogue.

Pillows are not needed for babies' beds. Babies can suffocate on a soft surface, since they don't have the strength to push themselves away. And pillows can hurt a growing baby's posture. If you buy a bedding set that includes a pillow, use it only for decoration.

OTHER NURSERY FURNITURE

When decorating the baby's room, parents often buy a set of nursery furniture as a package. But if you want to save money, avoid this temptation. The best buy on a crib from one manufacturer, for example, doesn't necessarily mean all other pieces in that line will be equally good buys. Use a critical eye to find better value.

An elaborate nursery suite that is outgrown within a year is a real extravagance. Consider every piece's adaptability. How will it look in an older child's room? Is the style too "babyish" for a four-year-old? Some manufacturers such as Little Folks, Morigeau, and Lepine offer matching suites where you can buy the crib and dresser at first, then buy the bed and other pieces when the child is older. Manufacturers keep them in their line for up to 10 years, but it's wise to check how long the suite has been available and if there's a chance of it being discontinued. Ask the store to keep your name on file and contact you if it is going to be phased out. Most manufacturers give plenty of notice.

Mixing and matching may work better as a decorating approach. A wall unit, for instance, could house baby's toys and toiletries now, display books and beetles and baseball cards later. What pieces promise the most mileage? Which styles are you least likely to grow tired of?

Don't restrict yourself to infants' departments when you shop for nursery furniture like dressers, chairs, etc. You may find better buys and simple, clean design in the standard furniture shops. A nursery doesn't need special baby furnishings to make its identity clear; you can do that with accessories. Forget about traditional uses for furniture and try to picture a piece's potential in your child's room. Would a loveseat work as a comfortable spot to relax with the baby? What about a plush armchair? (A rocking chair is practically *de rigueur* but check that it really *is* comfortable. Without good cushioning, a rocker can be too hard to sit on for any length of time.)

Dutailier Inc. of Montreal makes a wood-frame Glider Chair ($300 to $400, depending on upholstery) that is extremely popular because of its comfort.

The baby's dresser should be sturdy and well built, so you can continue to use it in your child's room after the crib has been folded up or passed on. It should meet several kinds of storage needs, with small drawers for tiny socks and T-shirts, deep drawers for bulky blankets and sweaters, maybe a built-in closet for hanging clothing.

For safety's sake, try to find a dresser with built-in drawer stops. These will prevent a child from pulling out the drawers and overturning the dresser. An adult can yank out the drawers with a good pull, but a child can only pull them out far enough to remove clothing or replace it.

Many dressers now have diaper changing areas on top, a design that may save space but won't save you any money. The changing surface often costs an extra $100 to $130, compared to $60 or $70 for a free-standing changing table. (Or you can buy or make your own vinyl-covered foam pad and attach it to the top of your child's dresser.) Young Generation sells a dresser with a built-in changing table that can later be used as a storage drawer.

A diaper changing table is not an essential and many parents do very well without one. But those who buy one find they use it constantly during the first year for diapering, dressing, and drying off after the bath.

Changing tables are the right height for an adult, waist-level so you can make diaper changes without awkwardly stooping. When no longer needed for diapers, the table can be used for stacking toys, for plants, as a television or stereo stand, even as a wine rack.

If you do buy a changing table, bypass the ones with a built-in bath. The design is quite impractical. "A mother will use this gadget about three or four times before she gets fed up with lugging water and resorts to a plastic tub on the kitchen or bathroom counter for washing her baby," says Catherine Scott, owner of Dear-Born Baby Furnishings in

Toronto. "Babies are a lot easier to carry than a tub full of water."

Since the tops of changing tables are made of vinyl, they eventually crack and discolour. You can protect your table top with a washable terrycloth cover (about $8) or a pillowcase. When the baby makes a mess, simply peel off the cover and replace it, leaving the table clean and ready for another quick diaper change.

Changing tables are convenient, but they can be dangerous if the child is left unattended. Babies, even when strapped in, can wriggle off a changing table when a parent's back is turned. Hospitals report that falls from changing tables are one of the biggest causes of injury to newborns. So if you hear the telephone or the doorbell ring while you're changing diapers, pick up the baby and take her with you.

NURSERY ACCESSORIES

Lighting is an easily forgotten element in nursery decorating but it's important nonetheless. Remember to buy a lamp, a night-light, or a dimmer switch for the overhead light—you want to be able to check on the baby at night without waking her.

Curtains, window shades, or venetian blinds are also worthwhile. They give the nursery a finished look and if they block the morning sun they may help your baby sleep a little later. Window shades come in solid colours but you can also find them in bright patterns or with bold graphics. Some shades co-ordinate with bedding and wallpaper.

If you're reluctant to wallpaper the entire nursery, why not buy borders instead? These are wide bands of patterned wallpaper that you can rim the top edges of the walls with, or place anywhere you would like to add some colour or contrast. It can accent the nursery's decor without overwhelming it. You can also use borders to co-ordinate with nursery wallpaper.

Don't forget to buy separate containers for laundry and dirty diapers. You can also purchase canvas organizers, which are wall hangings with small pouches for storing nursery needs like toiletries and diapers. You can hang one near the changing table or the crib.

Another useful accessory is an intercom system that allows you to get away from the nursery from time to time, but stay in touch. With a nursery intercom, you can be aware of baby's every sound as you move through the house or even go outdoors. Fisher-Price's Nursery Monitor and Gerry Deluxe Baby Intercom (both $55 to $60) are like one-way walkie-talkies and transmit sounds from the baby's room. You hear the baby through a receiver that you clip onto your belt or place somewhere nearby. Some newer models are two-way intercoms so you can talk to the baby from another room. But they are not babysitters — don't rely on them too much.

Mobiles are an established part of nursery furniture now. A musical mobile hung over the crib (about $30) will help soothe your infant at naptime and bedtime. A hanging mobile over the changing table will distract your child while you're changing her. But don't let mobiles dangle too low — they can be a hazard if the baby becomes entangled in them. And be sure to remove the mobile from the crib once the baby can pull herself up.

For a fantasy look in the nursery, add a colourful Chinese kite, vivid silky banners, or a collection of wallhangings. You can find wallhangings portraying all manner of designs: storybook characters, sunrises and skyscapes, fanciful animal farms.

CHAPTER 3

The First Weeks

LIFE AT HOME in the first weeks with a new baby is a busy, hectic period, full of excitement but also demanding, as you need time to recover from childbirth. Your newborn baby requires constant care, and while you struggle to adjust, you're flooded with visits and phone calls from friends and family.

Making the transition effortlessly is probably impossible. But you can take some steps to look after the baby's immediate needs, without neglecting your own. This chapter shows you how to provide the basics for baby — and a few essentials for you and your partner.

THE LAYETTE

You probably won't have to buy many new clothes at first because you'll be showered with gifts and hand-me-downs from friends and relatives. Newborn outfits are plentiful at secondhand stores and in great condition too. Babies grow so fast that they're in and out of sizes within a few weeks. Their first clothing has such a short life that it doesn't make sense to splurge. Save your shopping sprees for the time when the baby is old enough to wear clothing more than once or twice.

LAYETTE CHECKLIST

- ☐ 12 terrycloth sleepers or flannelette nightgowns
- ☐ 6 cotton undershirts
- ☐ 3 sweaters
- ☐ 3 bonnets
- ☐ 6 pairs socks or booties
- ☐ bunting bag with legs (for car seats and strollers)
- ☐ diaper bag
- ☐ disposable diapers *or* 3–4 dozen cloth diapers *or* a diaper service (80–100 per week)
- ☐ 3–4 dozen pairs plastic pants (if using cloth diapers)
- ☐ 8–10 receiving blankets
- ☐ 4 crib-sized blankets
- ☐ 6 crib sheets
- ☐ 6 carriage/bassinet-sized sheets
- ☐ waterproof changing pad
- ☐ disposable nurser kit *or* eight 8-ounce, four 4-ounce bottles with nipples and caps *or*, for breastfeeding, 2 to 4 bottles with nipples and caps plus nursing pads, breast pump
- ☐ toiletries (baby powder, baby lotion, towels, washcloth, baby soap, petroleum jelly, baby scissors, rectal thermometer, diaper wipes, diaper pins)

And if gift-givers ask what you would prefer, suggest they buy large sizes.

One hundred percent cotton is the fabric of choice for most parents. Unlike synthetics, cotton clothes breathe. They also wash better, don't retain odours and are softer for babies with sensitive skin. But cotton may not be allowed in some sleepwear because of flammability regulations.

Carter's is a reliable brand in cotton T-shirts. Snugabye

makes excellent sleepers and Absorba has a well-made line of French-imported diaper sets in simple, charming patterns.

Canadian designers are also bringing a fresh look to babywear. In Toronto, Irene Dale Designs are popular for their pretty prints and inventive styling. Milton Funwear, by Montreal's Milton Selections, is a range of infant and children's fashions with a make-believe theme. (Their panda sleepers are sold with a matching panda puppet.) Most baby boutiques carry small but distinctive lines of infant wear. You can find airbrushed T-shirts and dozens of other imaginative items for baby.

Cut down on your laundry by making sure you have plenty of nightgowns and sleepers in your baby's wardrobe. Babies need several changes of clothing a day. The more clothes you have, the less laundry you'll have to do. Try to keep this chore down to every other day or less, or you'll spend more time in the laundry room than you spend with the baby.

If you're lucky enough to have a summer baby, you can make do with a very small wardrobe of infant separates. On hot July and August days, a T-shirt and diaper are all your baby needs. If the weather turns cooler or a wind blows up, you can swaddle him in blankets to shield him from the breeze.

Blankets are considered a form of clothing in the first few months. They not only keep the newborn baby warm, but they enclose him and make him feel secure. Keep several blankets or shawls on hand, as well as a half-dozen cotton receiving blankets for wrapping the baby.

For babies born in cooler months, warmth is very important. It can even affect his mood. A baby who is uncomfortable with the temperature in the house will be fretful and fussy. Babies don't adjust as easily as adults do to hot and cold; they don't store heat well and they have less fat insulation. A baby is over six months old before he is able to shiver (which increases his body temperature). Instead, he produces heat by crying, kicking, and wriggling.

...and for my
next number...

**OTHER TIPS ON BUYING CLOTHES FOR
THE NEWBORN BABY:**

- Avoid clothes that button in the back. You don't want to turn the baby over to do all the fastening.

- Avoid clothes that have tight elastic bands at the arms or legs.

- Inspect the inside of all clothing to make sure the seams are soft, not scratchy. Check for pins or wires from price tags. Check for loose threads.

- Avoid lacy shawls or cardigans. The baby's fingers can be caught in the holes.

- If the garment is in a package, open it before buying to check the size. One maker's large may be another one's small. Don't trust the label alone.

- One-piece stretch sleepers are convenient, but they shouldn't fit tightly. (If you find later that the sleepers are too short but fit otherwise, cut off the feet and sew longer socks or booties to the bottoms.)

- Look for snowsuits or bunting bags with hoods and mittens attached. This eliminates the need for separate hats and mittens.

- Buy a few cotton bibs to save baby's clothes.

Parents often wonder how to dress the newborn. Is he wearing too many clothes, or not enough? Use your own comfort as a yardstick. In the daytime, if you only need lightweight clothing indoors, then so does he. Heavy layers of clothing in a warm sunny house will only make him sticky and irritable. But at night, make sure he's protected from drafts and put him to sleep in a drawstring nightgown or terrycloth sleepers that will keep his feet cosy if he wriggles out of his covers.

When buying clothes for the newborn, remember to check the diaper area. Do you have to remove the entire outfit before you can change the baby? Look for snaps or zippers along the legs, which allow quick diaper changes. Any other design is absurd.

BEST GIFTS

Here's what some parents singled out as gifts they especially appreciated:

- "A giant bunting bag for the stroller. It was a kind of cuddly sleeping bag, with no arms or legs. I used it for a season-and-a-half, and when Michaela was bigger and wore a snowsuit I could still zip her up in the bag. It was really warm and wind resistant, great during the winter."

- "Two toys: a handmade wooden castle and a wooden ironing board."

- "A Fisher-Price bib. It was soft and washable, with a Velcro closing and a front pocket. We used it till it was practically in pieces, then bought another."

- "A Tubbie — an inflatable ring. It was easy to bathe her in when she was just tiny and it was also a bed when we travelled with her. A great invention."

- "An Aprica stroller. It's lasted two years and it's still going strong."

- "A bottle sterilizer. I didn't think I needed it because I was breastfeeding, but when I went back to work we used it all the time for supplementary bottles. It was much easier than sterilizing all the bottles, caps, nipples, etc., separately."

Sizing in babywear is inconsistent. Some manufacturers use height and weight measurements, the most helpful system. Some use age measurements, which are misleading because they rarely reflect your child's real size—a three-month-old baby can wear a nine-month size. And some use small, medium, and large: sizes which are meaningless without a common standard.

Whatever the sizing system, look for garments that will fit until your baby is at least two or three months old. And since cotton garments shrink when washed, buy a size or two larger to begin with.

Don't forget to launder new baby clothes before they are worn for the first time, to remove the sizing. For your baby's laundry, you may want to buy a mild soap like Ivory Snow instead of the standard detergents that can irritate delicate skin. A stain remover or presoak liquid is a worthwhile investment too. And stock up on baking soda—it's great for removing odours from baby clothes. Just dab it on with a wet cloth or sponge.

BATHING YOUR BABY

"The tub bath is apt to be frightening at first to the inexperienced parent," says the legendary Dr. Spock. "The baby seems so helpless, limp and slippery, especially after being soaped." You'll know exactly what he means when you give your baby his first bath.

To ease your nerves, you can give the baby a sponge bath on top of a changing table or drawer at first. In fact, you can do it this way for months—until your child can sit up, if you prefer.

Parents often buy a small plastic baby bathtub (about $8 to $25), but this is an item you can live without. Babies outgrow a portable tub in three to six months. Meanwhile, you won't enjoy filling it up in the bathroom and hauling it somewhere else. (A water-filled tub is surprisingly heavy.)

Baby tubs are now better designed for bathing an infant, with slanted support areas for the baby and non-slip surfaces, but they aren't as practical as other options.

Some baby baths are designed to straddle an adult tub. One of these, the Jolly Bather (about $25), attaches securely to both sides of the tub and allows you to have your own bath with your infant supported on top. Others are designed to fit standard single or double kitchen sinks. Fisher-Price has one. (Measure your sink before you buy one of these. It's easy to get one that doesn't fit.)

The Bath-Eze is a popular invention with a low price tag (about $5). It's a washable cotton sling on an angled wire frame, which supports the baby in the bath while freeing your hands for soaping and rinsing. You can buy replacement covers when yours starts to disintegrate.

Another choice is the Tubbie (about $10), an inflatable tub which looks like a miniature wading pool. Babies often take to these, and you can use it for at least six months. Many parents like to take them along when they travel, to serve as a portable bed, although there is a danger of smothering.

You can also bathe the baby in the kitchen or bathroom sink. Make sure the taps are out of reach of the baby's kicking feet; if they're not, wrap the taps in a cloth or towel for safety. A plastic basin is an alternative, placed on a kitchen table or counter.

If you prefer the bathroom — and your back can stand the strain — you can place a small plastic tub inside the adult bathtub. An infant seat, with a towel replacing the pad, works well too. Or you might like to rest the baby on a two-foot sponge, the Bath Aid by Totkins, about $7.

Even with a portable tub and just a few inches of water, never leave the baby unattended. Take the phone off the hook during bath time so you won't be tempted to run off and answer its ring. Remember to keep all necessities, such as soap, shampoo, washcloth, and towels, close at hand so you don't have to step away from the tub while your baby is in it.

You can buy a bath thermometer to check the water temperature, but it's not necessary. Your wrist or elbow will give you a good reading. (Your hand isn't a reliable thermometer. It can convince you the water is cooler than it really is.) Always turn off the cold water last after you fill the tub, so the metal faucet will be cool and no hot water will drip into the tub.

When washing the baby's hair and scalp, use a baby shampoo so it won't sting his eyes as much as the ordinary kind. And instead of soap, which can dry out an infant's delicate skin, you may want to try a special liquid soap by Johnson & Johnson that is added to the water and doesn't need to be rinsed off. Or use a pump dispenser instead of bar soap, so you can keep one hand on the baby.

After the bath, your baby will like to snuggle into a hooded towel to be patted dry. (Babies lose a lot of heat through their heads, especially after their hair is shampooed.) Absorba makes a bath set: a hooded towel and a hooded bath bag that zips down the front. And a vinyl apron, with pockets for shampoo and soaps, will keep *you* dry while you bathe the baby.

You don't need to dust your baby with talcum powder after the bath—it dries out the skin. If you do use baby powder, don't shake it directly over the baby—the talc in the powder can harm the lungs. Shake it into the palm of your hand and pat it over the baby's skin. Cornstarch is an inexpensive substitute for baby powder and is safe to breathe. Johnson & Johnson, famous for baby powder, now make baby cornstarch as well. For more information on bathtime products for the older baby, see Chapter 4.

FIRST AID FOR PARENTS

During the first weeks at home, you'll spend most of your time either taking care of the baby or frantically trying to catch up on lost sleep. If the baby's father arranges to take some paternity leave or vacation time now and joins you at home, you can share the first week or two with the new baby. Many mothers find that this option is a life-saver. Both parents learn the basics of baby care together and coping with new parenthood seems easier when there are two to struggle with babyshock.

There will be little time for housework now. While your partner can take over most of the household chores, extra help may be necessary. It's best to arrange this before the baby arrives, since you need time to ask around for names, talk to agencies, place ads, and check references.

If a close friend or relative is willing to help out, take advantage of the offer. Even a daily visit of an hour or two, to do some laundry, make a meal, or let you nap, can be an enormous favour.

Some new mothers (especially if they are breastfeeding) find it practical to hire a temporary housekeeper. The housekeeper takes over the home front while the mother can concentrate on baby care only.

Be specific about the duties you want your household help to perform and prepare a list so there are no misunderstandings. These duties may include caring for the new baby, preparing meals, doing laundry (the baby's and yours), answering the telephone, greeting guests, preparing snacks for visitors, cleaning up the kitchen, light housekeeping, and grocery shopping.

Weekly cleaning help is an excellent idea for a new mother. It will control the domestic chaos which is usually one of the side effects caused by a new baby in the household.

If you can't afford professional help, you may find a student willing to do household chores for a small fee. A teenager can also do some light babysitting—for example, looking after the sleeping baby while you take a long, leisurely bath.

Stock up on groceries, ideally before the baby is born— especially frozen dinners, convenience foods, and easy-to-prepare meals. Even if you don't normally eat this stuff, you'll be glad of it when you have no time to cook. If you have take-out food stores nearby, take advantage of them.

For perishables such as fruit and vegetables, find a store that will deliver to your home. It's worth paying a few extra dollars to avoid the hassle of standing in checkout lines with a fussy baby.

If you can't face the kitchen, send out for food — especially when visitors arrive. Don't feel that you have to give them a home-cooked meal. Make a list of your favourite delivery places for pizza, chicken, and Chinese food, and keep their numbers by the phone.

Buy lots of film for your camera, so you can capture your baby's first moments of life. You'll want to photograph all your relatives and friends holding the baby, as well as every wardrobe change the baby makes. Smitten with love for your new family member, you'll probably take far more pictures than you expect, so don't skimp on film. Remember to buy a thick album for all your photos.

Keep a notebook with you in the hospital to record the presents you are given and, if you feel energetic, start sending out thank-you notes right away. (Buy stationery before the baby is born.) Use your notebook to record questions and answers, and to jot down your feelings and impressions about the baby and your new role as parent.

A baby record book is another must. You can note all the vital information about his birth and milestones in his development — the day he cut his first tooth, the first time he slept through the night, and so on. This baby book will become a treasured possession in later years, both for you and your child. If you can't find a book you like, buy a blank notebook or scrapbook and make your own.

Every new mother feels the need to escape occasionally, and to share her reactions to motherhood with other women. Check out classes for new mothers. Ask your prenatal teacher, your doctor, the nurses in your hospital, and your friends, if they know of any support groups you might join. The first weeks at home, we can't emphasize enough, are difficult and demand a period of adjustment. A group of mothers sharing the same experience, and a sympathetic instructor who has some answers, can do you a world of good. Most communities offer such programs. If yours doesn't, try contacting a few new mothers in the neighbourhood and forming your own self-help group.

You and your partner may start to feel housebound in this initial period. Indulge yourselves. Rent a video recorder and enjoy a movie night, or subscribe to pay television for a while. Upgrade your sound system and buy some new records. Order in a gourmet dinner and eat it by candlelight after the baby is asleep.

One couple with a new baby made an occasion out of Saturday nights. "I would buy a take-out meal from a nearby gourmet food shop," says Boyd, 36. "We would put Jonathan to bed at about 8 p.m. and enjoy dinner together on our own."

Once you are willing to leave the baby with a trusted babysitter, start venturing into the outside world again. Go out for the evening — or for just a few hours. Dinner in your favourite restaurant or a browse through the local bookstore can be a much-needed break from 24-hour parenting.

CHAPTER 4

First-Year Baby Gear

A CRIB OR CRADLE and a car seat are all the equipment you need at first, but other items come in handy later on. An infant seat provides the baby with a welcome change of perspective and a larger view of the world. An automatic swing soothes a fretful infant, while a doorway jumper provides entertainment and exercise. A playpen can free you temporarily for minor chores (while functioning as an extra crib), and a high chair is a better place than your lap to feed the baby once she can sit up.

You don't have to buy all these items, of course. Many can be borrowed or found reasonably priced at secondhand stores. And remember that what is essential to one family may not be to another. It all depends on how much room you have, your baby's temperament, your budget, and your lifestyle.

An automatic swing, for example, is a costly frill for some parents, a $50 to $100 pacifier that's used for only a few months and then becomes a white elephant. For others, it's a must. The first few months of babyhood are usually the toughest, for parents and babies alike, and if the swing helps to shorten their young infant's fussing episodes, most parents couldn't care less if the swing is obsolete later. While it's needed, it's worth its weight in gold.

INFANT CARRIERS AND BOUNCE CHAIRS

An infant carrier — a baby-sized chair made from moulded vinyl — gives a fresh new perspective to a baby who can't sit up alone. She can view the world around her instead of staring at the ceiling as she would in a crib or bassinet. It's useful from birth to six or seven months, until the baby becomes too active to sit still and grows heavy enough to tip it over. You can use it for feeding, for trips to the grocery store (some carriers fit nicely into the front of the shopping cart) and for bathing.

If you have a car seat, especially one that reclines, you can use it inside the house as an infant carrier. The same seat can do double duty. But an infant carrier *cannot* replace an approved car seat. There is no effective way to attach it securely to the car and it is not designed to withstand the impact of a crash.

Infant carriers with handles are easier to carry. The handle can often be hooked over the top of a chair, giving added stability for feeding. Deluxe infant carriers offer other features like feeding trays, detachable footrests, pouches to store diapers or bottles, and built-in music boxes.

We recommend buying an infant carrier with a rocker. When the baby is cranky, you can rock the chair and calm her down. (Rocked long enough, the baby may eventually doze off.) You may discover it's the secret of peaceful mealtimes — with your child perched atop the kitchen table in her carrier, you can rock her while you eat.

You can also buy a bounce chair, a metal frame with a fabric sling seat on which the baby reclines. These are also known as exercisers. The frame is flexible enough to provide a bouncing motion as the baby moves her arms or legs and this sensation really delights her.

A bounce chair should always be used on the floor, rather than a counter or table. Since it moves as it bounces, it could easily creep to the edge and fall off.

Bounce chairs are available in a wide choice of brands or styles. Some parents complain that the corduroy and canvas covers on bounce chairs soil easily, so check the chair's fabric before you buy.

Infant seats start at $15 and go up to about $40. Cheaper seats are lightweight and easy to tip, while more expensive seats offer better stability. The $30 Cradlemate, made by Cosco, has a pedestal base that is steadier than a metal or plastic stand. It also has a push-button adjustment.

Look for versatility when you choose an infant seat. If you can carry it and also use it for feeding, it will be a definite convenience. Make sure it has several seating angles. This will allow you to vary the baby's position and take some of the weight off the end of her spine. See how easily it can be adjusted and whether it can be locked into place for safety.

Check for sturdy construction. For maximum security, the base of the chair should be wider than the seat itself and there should be a non-skid surface on the bottom. Is the carrier's seat belt effective? How simple is it to open? Is the chair too heavy to carry easily from room to room?

Don't forget about the carrier's cushioning. Vinyl seats wipe easily but in summer heat your baby may find vinyl sticky and uncomfortable next to her skin. A padded seat is an extra luxury and better-quality fabric won't wear out as fast. The Kanga-Rocka-Roo carrier includes a fabric pouch that tucks beneath the seat to hold extra supplies. You can buy either a plain Kanga-Rocka-Roo or one with extra uses. One model doubles as an infant swing seat, another as an infant car restraint.

Never leave your baby unattended in an infant carrier. No infant chair is impossible to tip. (To help prevent tipping, you can weight the metal stand in the back with a heavy book.) Always use the seat's belts or restraining straps.

A baby in an infant seat is much safer on the ground, where she won't be hurt if she does manage to flip the seat over. Always put the seat on the floor if you leave the room for even a moment. If the seat is on a table or countertop, get in the habit of keeping one hand on it if you must turn away, or use clamps to secure it. Take extra care when you are carrying your baby in an infant seat. Injuries to the baby have occurred when an adult has tripped or fallen with a carrier.

Some child-care experts dislike infant seats because they reduce the physical contact so necessary between parent and child. They also prevent her from reaching out, touching objects, and holding her head up. And some doctors feel that propping up an infant can aggravate digestive problems. The consensus is that a very young baby is better off spending most of the time on her stomach or back. If you buy an infant seat, use it sparingly and give your baby plenty of cuddling in between her lounging sessions.

AUTOMATIC SWINGS

Automatic swings are swings that hang from a free-standing frame and, once wound up, rock the baby for minutes at a time. They are a boon to many parents, who swear they couldn't have survived the first few months without one. "I don't know how parents used to manage before automatic swings were invented," says one grateful dad.

A cradle or rocking chair will swing the baby, but *you* have to do the work. Wind-up swings do the work for you. They last at least fifteen minutes at a stretch, and the new battery-powered models go for hours. Many a fretful baby falls under the swing's spell — that's why the swing is now an almost mandatory piece of nursery equipment.

If you plan to buy a swing, be sure you have plenty of space. Swings take up a lot of room, nearly as much as a playpen. And they are useful for a very short period, so try to borrow rather than buy.

Keep in mind, too, that there is no guarantee your child

will adore the swing. Some infants are unimpressed and even frightened or nauseated by the swinging motion. It's often smart to postpone this purchase until the baby is born, so you can give her a trial run.

You can put your child in a swing from the first day you bring her home, if you have the right model. Swings designed for newborns have a reclining seat or a cradle attachment. (The cradle attachment, however, costs an extra $20 to $25.) If you inherit a hand-me-down with an upright seat, you can prop up the baby with towels, blankets, or a head-hugger pillow. And if you want to take the swing outside on sunny days, you can buy a canopy (about $10) to shade her.

Most swings are designed to hold babies who weigh up to 11 kilograms (or 25 pounds), but your child may outgrow it before then. As soon as your baby can grasp the bars, stop using it.

If you buy a swing, don't get the old-fashioned kind that you wind up and allow to run down. Rewinding is so noisy that you can easily startle a near-dozing infant. Some manufacturers offer a silent wind-up feature, and this is often an essential, as many parents testify. The newer swings are battery-operated and provide a much longer ride. The Graco Non-Stop Swyngomatic (about $110) runs up to 150 hours on two alkaline "D" batteries, and has a variable speed control that lets you choose the speed best suited to your baby.

Automatic swings grow more sophisticated every year and the prices rise in direct proportion to their frills. You can buy a swing for $30, or one for $140. Cheaper models have a vinyl seat that does not recline. Higher-priced models have an adjustable, moulded plastic seat upholstered in vinyl or fabric. The cradle attachment costs more but it can serve as a bassinet too and has convenient carrying handles. Batteries, better-quality chairs and modern design increase the price.

When shopping for a swing, find out how much noise it makes and how long the ride lasts. Check the width of the legs and the space they take up. Does the frame collapse for storage? How easy is it to get the baby into and out of the seat? Is there a seat belt?

For safety's sake, the frame should be wide for better balance and less risk of tipping. Frames on some models have a brace between the legs for added stability. The legs should lock into place and the seat should attach securely to the frame. Be sure the legs have caps on the ends to protect your floors and reduce skidding.

Graco's Swyngomatic Swing/Infant Carrier has a removable reclining infant seat, comfortably cushioned in a washable fabric. The seat hooks up to the swing's frame when your baby needs a swinging session and unhooks to serve as a sturdy chair. Dorel, Fisher-Price and Swyngomatic also produce automatic swings. Evenflo has a four-position seat that can be unhooked from the swing and used as an infant car seat, and the Kanga Super Swing has a seat that can be lifted out to become a carrier.

A word of warning about automatic swings: use the seat belt, no matter how young your infant. And never, ever, leave your child alone in the swing.

WALKERS AND JUMPERS

Walkers have fallen out of favour. Health care professionals have become increasingly aware of the dangers baby walkers — baby chairs on wheels — pose. Infants have fallen down stairways and suffered concussions and crushed fingers in walkers that collapsed or tipped over. Hospitals across Canada report that hundreds of infant injuries, and even some deaths, are related to walker use.

Walkers are the single most common cause of head injuries in children under one year of age. More than half of walker accidents involve falls on stairways. Children hurtle down the steps and land at the bottom, with the walker on top of them.

Serious falls don't require a long flight of stairs, either.

One baby fell down only three steps in her walker, yet suffered a fractured skull.

Do you *need* a walker? Absolutely not. Although they are handy, they don't provide a real benefit. Doctors say there is no evidence that the use of a walker improves co-ordination or has any other developmental advantages. In fact, a baby who relies on a walker may take longer to start walking on her own.

Consumer and Corporate Affairs Canada has developed a voluntary set of safety rules for walkers, taking effect in 1989. The new walkers should be larger than the width of a standard door to prevent babies from getting out of a room and onto stairs. Also, warning labels will be attached prominently, reminding parents never to leave a child unattended.

"One thing is clear," says the Canadian Institute of Child Health, an Ottawa-based lobby group. "Parents and caregivers need to be aware that walkers do pose a very real threat to a child's safety." The group feels voluntary standards are not enough to prevent accidents.

A baby walker looks innocent enough. It gives mobility to children who are still unsteady on their feet, allowing them to expand their horizons and explore the world from an upright position. And a walker is a convenient place for the baby to sit up, eat, or play.

But the danger lies in lack of supervision. Often parents are occupied with other chores while the baby is in the walker. At such times, a baby can race to an open stairway and tumble, walker and all, down a flight of stairs.

Infants in walkers are extremely mobile. "It has been estimated that a baby in a walker can cover one metre in one second," says a 1984 study by three London, Ontario, doctors, published by the *Canadian Medical Association Journal*. "This outpaces the reaction time of the occupied parent."

To determine how often falls involved baby walkers, the three doctors sent questionnaires to families with children aged three months to eighteen months. Of 152 families responding, a shocking 36 percent — more than one out of three — reported that their child had had a fall while in a walker. Most of the falls were in the six-month to nine-month age group.

The more time a baby spent in a walker, the more likely the baby was to fall. Of the children who had a walker-related fall, 54 percent spent more than two hours a day in the walker. Unfortunately, the product is all too often treated like a babysitter. Three-quarters of parents questioned by the doctors said they used a walker to keep the baby quiet and happy.

If a walker is used, the time spent in it should be limited, preferably to thirty minutes per day, recommended the study. Walkers should be used on a home's lowest floor and never near open stairways. "A loose-fitting gate may provide false security," they emphasized.

Even when there is no hazard from stairs, walkers pose a threat to infants. Propped upright and mobile, they can reach for poisonous plants, dangling electrical cords, hot liquids, or pots and pans. Babies in walkers have a higher incidence of burns and poisonings than other infants.

"It's like giving a teenager a convertible," says Dr. Elizabeth Hillman, a pediatrician at the Janeway Child Health Centre in St. John's, Newfoundland. Two infants there were severely scalded while their parents were preparing formula in the kitchen. They manoeuvred their walkers to the boiling kettle, reached for the electric cord, and poured hot water down on themselves.

A walker is not a substitute for the development of crawling and walking skills. Your child's leg motion in a walker is different from the motion she'll use for walking, and if she relies on the walker too much, she may learn to walk later than usual. A baby placed in a walker at too young an age — before she can sit, let alone toddle — can have such weak muscle tone in her legs that she has to tiptoe to get the walker moving. She may take longer than average to develop a normal gait. It's important to choose an appropriate age for a walker's use, preferably when the baby is already able to move herself about on her own. Six months is a good age and your baby shouldn't be using a walker past twelve months.

Constantly supervise your child while she is in a walker. It's the key to preventing accidents. The new federal standards, when enacted, will ensure that walkers are sturdy and stable and won't tip easily. But no matter how safe its design, a walker should never be used as a babysitter.

If you are buying a walker, look for a wide tip-resistant base and a height that can be adjusted as your baby grows. See if the seat is well padded and has a high back. (A high back with padding may help reduce neck injuries if an accident throws the baby back against the seat.) Find out if it collapses and also locks in place for safety. Does it have a locking device to prevent accidental folding?

The safest walker is Dorel's Baby Tyme ($35 to $40), which has lockable wheels. This "stay put" feature, as it's called, allows you to keep the baby in one place if necessary. A walker which doesn't *go* anywhere is not really a walker, some might argue, but it's a safe device nonetheless.

When you use the walker, always keep doors closed and stairways blocked. Use safety gates where possible. Stick to flat, smooth surfaces, away from carpet edges and other obstructions. Get rid of throw rugs. Be sure that all small toys that could trip up the walker are removed from the floor, and that no hanging objects such as appliance cords and purse straps are available to small fingers. Never allow your baby to go near the fireplace, the stove, or any other source of heat.

Walkers, despite their potential dangers, remain popular with some parents and babies. One mother finds the walker handy for travel. "Ours was collapsible and it doubled as a high chair." Her daughter enjoyed her walker and since it was too wide to fit through doorways her mobility was limited. They had no mishaps.

The jumper is an alternative to a walker for fun and exercise—a fabric seat suspended on a spring that hangs from a door frame or from its own stand. The baby is harnessed into the seat and then can bounce and leap and revel in her temporary super-baby powers.

A jumper can be used once the baby can sit well (about six months) and until she learns to walk. Start using a jumper when your baby weighs at least 6 kilograms (about 14 pounds), and stop when she reaches 10 kilograms (25 pounds). The peak period for their popularity is before the baby begins to crawl. Expect to pay about $30 for a doorway jumper and $50 for a freestanding one.

Jumpers have provoked the same barrage of criticism as walkers. Some child-care experts charge that they discourage the development of motor skills and can cause injury to growing bones. But there are no studies that prove that jumpers are harmful or helpful to babies. Discuss the pros and cons of jumpers with your child's doctor before you buy.

If you are buying a doorway jumper, check that the door moulding at home is sturdy enough to hold the weight of the baby as she bounces. If you're not sure about the strength of your door frame, buy a stand with its own frame (but remember, it will cost more and take up far more room).

Like the walker, a doorway jumper should be used for only brief periods and always under supervision. A baby can hit her head on the door frame or become trapped in the strings when trying to reach a toy. Find a doorway wide enough that the baby won't bang into it, and adjust the jumper so that the soles of her feet touch the floor. Check the clamp each time you attach the jumper for signs of breakage or wear. Head injuries have been caused when clamps have given way and sent baby and jumper to the floor.

Jolly Jumper is the well-known brand in jumpers but Evenflo offers a Johnny Jump-Up "gym-set" that is attractive in design. Fisher-Price has one called the Hop Skip Jumper, with a sturdy door frame locking clamp.

PLAYPENS

Mothers in the 1940s and 1950s used to keep their babies in playpens for long hours each day. A baby who accepted her playpen confinement was considered well disciplined; a baby who objected was spoiled.

Today, playpens aren't in vogue. They are seen as unnecessary, old-fashioned, and a way of trapping your child to save yourself work and aggravation. Child-rearing philosophies have seen radical changes in the years since the baby boomers sat obediently in their wooden cages. Now the boomers' own babies run free. More and more parents are babyproofing their homes, then unleashing their babies and closely supervising them. The playpen ends up in the corner of the living room, an overgrown toy box. Parents fling rattles, blocks, and stuffed animals into it, but the baby is rarely an occupant.

Recent studies have shown that babies confined to playpens show slower development than babies who are given the freedom to explore from the floor. Playpen babies also suffer from boredom.

Aware their product has an image problem, manufacturers have responded by liberating the playpen. No longer a prison, it's now a "play yard" — a fun place for baby to romp. Sizes are bigger and more varied, fabrics are bright and lively. Often toys are built right into the pens. The emphasis is on stimulation, not confinement.

Will *your* baby enjoy a playpen or play yard? It depends on how early and how often you use it. Although you don't need one until the baby begins to crawl, introduce it no later than three months after the baby is born. Set aside a specific period of time for the baby to play there, and stick to that schedule. Keep sessions short — no longer than an hour at a time.

A busy parent can find the playpen helpful. When the phone rings or there's housework to do, you can plunk the baby down and know she's safe for a few minutes. The playpen can be used outdoors, while you garden or concentrate on your suntan. Best of all, it can double as a crib when you travel.

Playpens have one disadvantage as a crib, however. The floor pad, usually a thin vinyl-covered piece of foam, provides little support. If you intend to use a playpen regularly for this purpose, look for one with a thick floor pad. (Bo Peep, Graco, Dorel, and Fisher-Price have introduced a playpen with a thicker pad, specifically designed for use as a travel crib.) Or invest in a good mattress and make sure it fits tightly, with no more than a 4-centimetre (1½-inch) gap between the mattress edges and the playpen walls.

There are three types of playpens. The older models with wooden frames and barred sides are coming back (St. Ferdinand has a new line), but most have metal frames and mesh sides which are lighter and more portable. Then there's the corral, a playpen with a flexible shape and no floorboard, which can be custom designed to suit your needs. This type is not popular except for outdoors.

Federal regulations for playpens, passed in 1976, ensure the mesh is small enough so that it can't catch fingers, toes or buttons. (Two infants choked to death when the buttons on their clothes became trapped in the jumbo mesh of their older playpens.) Mosquito-type netting is the type now used. Playpens cannot have more than two wheels or casters, so their movement is restricted. The sides must be at least 48 centimetres (or 19 inches) in height so the baby can't climb or fall out. No rough or sharp edges are allowed and hinges must be designed to prevent pinching.

A more recent safety hazard involves the drop sides on mesh playpens. When one side of the playpen is left down, the mesh sags into a loose pocket into which an infant can fall or roll and suffocate. After several baby deaths in the United

States, playpen manufacturers started modifying their designs. Now there are several models with no-drop sides, which can be folded easily with one hand. (If you have a mesh playpen with drop sides, *never* leave one side down — even when your child is not in the playpen. Both sides should always be locked into position.)

Also dangerous are wooden corrals, accordion-style enclosures that consist of wooden slats riveted together. When the enclosure is opened up, the slats form V-shaped openings at the top and diamond-shaped openings in the middle. These openings can trap children's heads and necks if they try to climb out of them. Manufacturers have voluntarily stopped production, but you may find an old wooden corral at a garage sale. Don't buy it.

Bigger is not necessarily better in playpens. The largest size, 100 centimetres by 100 centimetres, (40 inches by 40 inches), costs about $75 to $100 and takes up a lot of room. A slightly smaller playpen, 90 centimetres by 90 centimetres (36 inches by 36 inches), saves money (about $10) and floor space and will probably suit your purposes just as well.

Try collapsing the playpen you're planning to buy. Notice how much space it takes up. Will it fit into the luggage compartment of your car? The Houdini (about $60) is a 90-centimetre-by-90-centimetre playpen that folds like an umbrella into a long, thin shape, rather than flat and wide. Its portability has made it extremely popular.

The vinyl upholstery on mesh playpens should be strong enough to withstand chewing without tearing. (A teething baby can swallow a piece of vinyl and choke on it.) A good test for vinyl on playpens — or any other baby equipment — is to pinch the upholstery between your thumb and forefinger. If it pinches easily and seems thin and flimsy, try another brand.

Children should never be left unattended in playpens. Don't leave large toys inside, because they can be used as step stools for climbing out. When the baby is 34 inches (89 centimetres) tall or 30 pounds (about 14 kilograms)—about eighteen months old—it's time to put the playpen away.

Make safety checks of your playpen. You may discover loose parts which need repair. If you have an older playpen with wide mesh, never let your child inside if she's wearing clothing with buttons or hooks. They could become tangled in the mesh.

A few playpens feature vinyl "windows" that let your child look out at the world without the mesh obstructing her view. Others include activity centres permanently attached to their sides. These are appealing accessories, but they probably won't satisfy a child who hates the playpen anyway.

The Safe-T-Pen, about $80 to $90, is very lightweight and comes apart easily for storage in an attractive tote bag. But a test by Canadian Consumer magazine showed that the flexible sides are a potential danger to an older baby trying to climb out. It is best to buy a playpen with rigid side rails.

PLAYPEN DONT'S

- *Don't* leave your child unattended in the playpen.
- *Don't* tie toys to the playpen; they can cause strangulation.
- *Don't* leave a playpen's side down.
- *Don't* let your baby chew on a playpen's vinyl padding.
- *Don't* leave large toys in the playpen that could serve as stepping stones to help your baby climb out.

HIGH CHAIRS AND FEEDING TABLES

High chairs are an essential piece of baby furniture. Once your baby can sit up, she can perch in her high chair and join the family meals. She will use the high chair until she is at least eighteen months old, so this particular item needs to be a careful purchase.

Safety, quality, and practicality are the three major factors to keep in mind when you purchase a high chair. Bargain buys aren't recommended, because often they come at the expense of sturdy construction. It's also wise to select a high chair with an appearance you like, because it will be a kitchen fixture for many months to come.

The high chair you buy should be easy to clean. Babies have an uncanny ability to cover every inch of a high chair in food. More than any piece of baby equipment you acquire, this one needs the most scrubbing. So examine it for all-over washability; don't stop your inspection at the feeding tray. A chair with knobs and rungs, for example, will be harder to clean than a straight-legged model. Small nooks and crannies will harbour dried babyfood. Chair seats made from vinyl or plastic wipe clean, fabric upholstery doesn't.

Babies squirm, climb, and bounce in a high chair, so it needs to be solid and safe for their activity. If you need a high chair that folds away for storage, make sure you buy one that locks securely into place in the upright position.

Some collapsible models come with a double fold, which reduces them to the size of a small suitcase. These high chairs are ideal for use at the grandparents' or for travelling.

A safe high chair has legs that are set wide enough apart to be tip-proof. It comes equipped with a sturdy seat belt *and* a crotch strap to prevent your baby from sliding out. (Safety straps should not be attached to the tray in any way, so that you can remove the tray for cleaning.)

The tray should lock securely into place and you should be able to operate it with one hand. Avoid high chairs with trays that flip up when not in use. The tray can trap the baby's head as it swings down. A tray that swings to the side is preferable. Also, look for an adjustable tray with at least three positions. Even better is a locking system that adjusts to any position as the child grows. Some models have a tray that detaches completely, which allows you to push the high chair up to the table.

A wooden chair is not practical, though it is handsome. Eating utensils, abrasive cleaners, even the banging of a baby's toys, can damage the finish. Similarly, you may be charmed by an antique high chair, but not only is it probably hard to clean, it may be unsafe. Are the legs wide enough apart so that your baby can't topple it over? If you still prefer a wood chair, buy a washable cotton high chair pad (about $15) to guard against stains and nicks.

When shopping for a high chair, look for a tray that's deep and wide enough, with a lip to catch spills. Are the tray and the footrest adjustable? (Choose a tray that grasps the arm of the chair, rather than one where you must line up holes to a button.) Is the chair back high enough to support the baby's head?

The Rolls-Royce of high chairs is the Fisher-Price model. About $100, it is one of Canada's hottest sellers. The design combines practicality with a sleek modern style. Rated the top juvenile product of 1984 in the United States, the chair is in short supply in many Canadian stores. Among its features are a removable seat bottom for easy clean-up, raised elbow rests that keep the baby out of the babyfood, extra-wide legs, and a large ivory-coloured wraparound tray that can be operated with one hand. The chair's upholstery is padded vinyl in a posy-patterned fabric. A panel of parents in *Canadian Consumer* magazine recently gave top ratings to the Fisher-Price high chair, followed by Simmons' Little Folk Model.

Gerry's First Meal High Chair (about $100) has a seat that reclines to accommodate a newborn baby. This looks like a great idea at first, until you realize that you don't feed solids to a baby until she is four or five months old. At that age, the baby is starting to sit up and doesn't really need a reclining seat any more. (But you might want a high chair with a wingback or side support to keep the baby from slipping sideways.)

If you're planning to remove the tray and use the high chair directly at the table, be sure the arms will fit under your tabletop. Measure the height of your table and keep this in mind when you shop.

Many high chairs are designed to convert to other uses, such as a youth chair, rocking chair, adult utility chair, or play desk. Consider whether you need this flexibility and whether it's worth any extra cost.

An innovation in the high chair market is the portable seat that can be hooked onto any table. Particularly useful in restaurants or in small eating spaces, these clip-on chairs have metal frames with seats made of moulded plastic or durable nylon or canvas. Most models can hold a child up to 18 kilograms (or 40 pounds), the weight of an average four-year-old. Sassy Seat is one brand name. Another is Pansy Ellen's My Chair or Babydiner.

Portable clip-on chairs, which range from $15 to $30, cost much less than high chairs and take up far less storage space. But many parents prefer high chairs because they help contain the baby's messes. Since most portable chairs have no tray, the baby sits right at the table with you, ready to spill your food and hers with a single blow.

Test the stability of your table before putting your child in a hanging high chair. While it's attached to the table, place an object which weighs at least 18 kilograms (or 40 pounds) in the chair. If your table wobbles, don't use the portable chair on it. Dorel has a new clip-on high chair with an extra-strong lock. It's about $30 to $35, but certainly worth the extra few dollars.

Some hanging chairs include warnings that they are not safe for use on a glass table. Never attach the seat to a tableclothed surface—the tablecloth can slide right off the table, bringing the seat with it.

One mother reports that a portable chair has replaced her child's high chair in their household. "Originally we bought a 'Sassy Seat' to take into restaurants. But our daughter adored it so much that it's now permanently attached to the kitchen table. It causes less mess at mealtime because the arms stop her from dropping dishes on the floor. And she really likes being right at the table with us."

Whether you use a high chair or a hanging chair, never allow your child to stand up in it. It's not cute, it's dangerous. And do not leave your child unattended in the chair.

If you're using a high chair, don't depend on the tray to hold the baby in. Always double check to make sure the tray is locked into place. Keep the high chair out of high-traffic areas and away from kitchen appliances or other objects within the baby's reach. And don't lean a folded high chair against a wall, where it can be knocked down by a curious toddler.

Low chair-table combinations are safer than high chairs because they're closer to the floor and have a shorter, more stable base. If the baby is going to be eating most of her meals alone, this design is preferable. If, however, you plan to eat family-style at the kitchen table, your baby will be at a lower level, unable to participate in the fun of family meals.

Feeding tables are similar in design to walkers, but they're more stable. If there are wheels, they should lock into a stationary position. Feeding tables are usually more expensive than high chairs and not as widely available.

Silver Cross, England's pedigreed baby carriage company, makes an excellent high and low chair (about $120). In its upright position, it's a standard high chair. Horizontally, it is a safe, low feeding table. The major disadvantage is that it's difficult to manoeuvre the baby in and out of the chair. And as the tray is not adjustable it cannot be removed for easy clean-up. Also, unlike most high chairs, the Silver Cross does not have a harness.

If you do buy a feeding table, don't expect it to serve any other purpose. These tables are often promoted as being versatile and their ads may picture a happy toddler busy with paints and paper. But in reality a child hardly ever agrees to climb into these contraptions except at mealtimes.

As a substitute for a high chair when travelling or visiting, you can buy a cloth harness that fits onto a standard kitchen chair. The pillowcase design slips over the back of the chair and then ties around the baby's waist. Cloth harnesses are safe, inexpensive (Consumers Distributing sells the Travel Safety Seat for under $10), and easy to fold away in your diaper bag or purse. The Buggy Hugger by Formelco in Toronto is more expensive, but is made with two pieces for better fit and ties at the back with Velcro.

A harness can be used to secure a baby in a high chair with no safety straps, and some models can be useful for automatic swings and shopping carts.

A booster seat on top of a kitchen chair is also a substitute for a high chair, but only when the baby is a bit older. Most parents wait until a child is between fifteen and twenty-four months to introduce a booster seat and continue to use it until she's three or four years old.

A sturdy moulded-plastic booster seat costs about $15 to $20. Look for one with a non-skid surface and at least two seating heights. (Some models fold in half and are hinged to provide four seating levels.) If the seat does not have a safety strap, you can make one yourself with a belt or strap. To prevent tumbles, strap the booster seat to the chair, then strap your child to the booster seat.

Booster seats approved for use in the car can also be used in the kitchen, but not vice versa. Unless the booster seat has been specially designed and tested as a car seat, don't use it in your car.

BATH AIDS

Once your baby graduates to the grown-up bathtub, she must still be held carefully so she doesn't slip. If you want both hands free to bathe your baby, you'll need some sort of safety device to keep her secure in the tub.

The most common bathtime aid is a round or triangular plastic ring (about $10), which fits around the baby and supports her in the tub. It stays put with suction rings, though it may not stick properly if your tub has a rippled or roughened surface. The Jolly Bath Ring is one brand name for this item. A variation is a plastic chair without legs, cushioned and belted and held down with suction cups.

Both types are good investments, allowing you to sit by the tub while the baby plays instead of straining your back to hold onto her. You can start using either one when your child is able to sit up (about six months). The ring lets you bathe the baby easily, whereas you may find the chair's design awkward for reaching her back or bottom.

A bathtub spout cover will protect the baby from injury when she plays in the tub. You can buy a vinyl-coated foam cover that fits on any standard faucet (and has a friendly bear face) for $14.25, from the Born to Love catalogue. (For information on mail order catalogues, see Chapter 1.)

A shampoo shield can be a lifesaver for the parent. The shield keeps soap out of the baby's eyes while you wash her hair. Mothercare, Baby Love and Born to Love have an excellent one for about $5, a flexible plastic ring which slips over the child's head. If your child detests shampoos, this is just the item. (Shampoo shields are not a new product but they have been almost impossible to find until recently. Their comeback is long overdue.)

Once the baby can stand, you can buy a step stool to give her access to the bathroom sink. One model, made with wooden slats (about $15), doubles as a child's chair. Fisher-Price has a moulded plastic stool ($20), with cheerful Sesame Street graphics and child-sized handles for easy carrying. Some other names in step stools are Baby Bjorn (which comes with a three-year warranty) and Gendron Freedom Step.

CHAPTER 5

Diapers

BELIEVE IT OR NOT, you will be changing about 7,400 diapers in your child's first two-and-a-half years. You have three alternatives for your marathon diaper changes: disposables, cloth diapers, and diaper services.

DISPOSABLE DIAPERS

Disposables are the winners with Canadian parents. Over 75 percent of Canadian babies are diapered in disposable diapers.

The reason for their popularity is obvious. They are wonderfully convenient. Disposables can be tossed out into the garbage, their tape fasteners eliminate the need for safety pins and the plastic backing means that plastic pants aren't necessary either.

When disposables first appeared on the scene they were bulky and clumsy in shape, uncomfortable to wear and awkward to put on. As a further drawback, they required pinning, just like cloth diapers. The design has grown increasingly refined, however. Now there is an hourglass shape to some brands, along with a better fit and elasticized legs to prevent leaks.

Self-tapes have been improved too. They stick better and

are refastenable. (This solves a chronic problem disposable diapers had in the past. If you checked your child's diaper and found it was dry, you had to discard the clean diaper anyway or resort to strips of masking tape to fasten it again, since the adhesive tabs lost their stickiness.)

Pampers and Luvs, by Procter & Gamble, and Huggies, made by Kimberly-Clark, are the three well-known brand names in disposable diapers.

Huggies and Luvs, both high in price, have been locked in battle in the "diaper wars" over the last few years, as Procter & Gamble and Kimberly-Clark compete for sales. In the U.S., Huggies are winning so far but the margin is narrow.

With the introduction of new versions of Pampers and Luvs, however, the competition may grow tougher. And a Canadian consumer test rated the cheaper Pampers diaper as highly as the more expensive Huggies and Luvs, so price isn't always a guarantee of quality.

The major diaper makers are all coming out with new ultra-thin varieties, which contain a substance that absorbs liquid and turns it into a gel. There has been some controversy about the safety of this substance, called polyacrylate, but the Consumers' Association of Canada said it poses no health hazard, even if ingested orally. The group's lab tests showed that ultra-thin diapers were more absorbent than regular diapers in both day and nighttime use.

There are other brands of disposables, including house brands carried by grocery stores, department stores and drugstores. But quality varies and if the price is rock-bottom, be suspicious. It may indicate an inferior product. You may not like the fit or they may have poor absorbency, faulty tapes, or other flaws.

Try a few brands of disposable diapers to find out which diaper suits your baby best. Buy in small quantities. Don't stock up on any one brand until you know which one you like. Then take advantage of sales and buy in bulk. Drugstores, discount stores, and department stores have regular sales.

Avoid over-buying in the "newborn" size, however, since you don't know how long your child will fit into them.

If you're an urbanite, search out discount warehouses for low-priced disposables. You can buy disposable diapers by the pound and while a few will be flawed, most are perfect. The price is about 40 percent cheaper than brand-name diapers, so the savings are dramatic.

At the other extreme, services which deliver disposable diapers to your door are available in a few cities. Delivery is sometimes free with a minimum order of diapers.

The major hesitations parents voice about disposable diapers centre on expense, environmental concerns — and diaper rash. Disposables definitely cost more than cloth diapers. For the two-and-a-half years your baby is in diapers, you will pay $650 to $950 for cloth diapers, about $1,200 for a diaper service, and $2,000 for disposables. But convenience usually wins out over cost.

It's been estimated that the baby who is diapered exclusively in disposables produces a half-ton of garbage in the period from birth to toilet-training age. The plastic on these diapers is not bio-degradable and disposables are rarely disposed of properly, adding to solid waste. Again, convenience often outweighs environmental convictions. But if it doesn't in your case, use recyclable cloth diapers.

Most parents simply dump a dirty disposable diaper into the garbage. But disease organisms can be present on a dirty diaper. They pose a health hazard. The best way to discard a disposable is to shake it clean over the toilet and tie it up in a plastic bag before you throw it into the trashcan. Never flush a disposable diaper down the toilet. Despite what it may say on the box, the inner lining alone can plug up the plumbing.

Diaper rashes are more likely with babies who use disposable diapers. They can be minimized, however. Experiment with different brands until you find one your baby is comfortable in. Babies are sometimes sensitive to the perfume used in disposables, and this can result in rashes. Cheaper brands of disposables — house brands, for example — are sometimes perfume-free.

Rashes may also be caused by the plastic backing, which prevents air circulation and seals in the moisture; more importantly, the plastic covering makes it harder to tell that the baby needs changing so diaper changes are often less frequent. Check the baby regularly. Reusable tabs make this precaution more practical.

DIAPER SERVICE

Diaper services provide a weekly supply of clean cotton diapers, delivered to your door. This alternative is more economical than disposable diapers, more convenient than washing your own diapers. And as one diaper-service advocate says, "Even if a service is more expensive, I figure it's the least we can do to give the environment a break."

Fresh diapers are dropped off at your home and your baby's soiled ones are picked up and laundered. The services add bacteriostats (which stop bacteria growth that causes odour and rashes) during rinsing so that you don't even have to rinse the used diaper before placing it in the pail. The laundering process includes softeners and rinsing agents that reduce soap residue and the diapers are completely sterilized.

A diaper service will provide you with a diaper pail, deodorizer, and a bag for soiled diapers. Weekly deliveries of eighty diapers cost $12 to $15 and for a small extra fee (approximately 25¢ for ten) you can increase your order.

Order heavily at first (ninety diapers or more), so you'll have all the diapers you need. Extras can be used for wiping spills and protecting your clothes from the baby.

While you're pregnant, check the Yellow Pages for listings of diaper services and ask about prices. (Some companies give discounts if you register before the baby is born and they deliver the first shipment of diapers about a week before your due date.) If you prefer, you can call from the hospital to say when you want the service to begin. Ask them if they supply waterproof pants or diaper covers. If they don't, stock up on a dozen or so pairs.

CLOTH DIAPERS

If you plan to use your own diapers, you will need four to six dozen, along with a diaper pail (preferably a lock-top style), and waterproof pants. Diaper pins are optional.

Cloth diapers come prefolded, fitted, or flat. The most common fabrics are gauze, bird's eye (similar to dishtowel material), and flannel. Mothercare-by-Post, the English catalogue of baby goods, sells terrycloth "nappies." Each of these materials has advantages. Bird's eye and terrycloth are the most absorbent, gauze is the lightest and most airy, flannel is the most comfortable on a baby's skin.

Babykins, developed by two mothers in Richmond, B.C., have a Velcro fastening system that allows them to be adjusted to fit from newborn to the toilet training stage. They are available from department stores and specialty shops for $70 a dozen. There is also the Sweetheart diaper, which you can buy or sew yourself from a pattern.

Prefolded cloth diapers eliminate the chore of folding, but laundering diapers is still time-consuming. Think it over carefully before you decide to wash diapers at home. You will be swamped with baby's laundry anyway: sleepers, vests, receiving blankets, and so on. Add a daily heap of diapers that must be washed separately — and carefully, with special detergents, bleaches, and softeners — and you'll have little time left over.

If you prefer all-natural cotton diapers to disposables, the compromise of a diaper service will save you time and energy. Even if you choose cloth diapers, it's good to have some disposable diapers on hand. Disposables are more convenient when you're travelling or visiting.

Cheap plastic pants are not a smart buy. They harden and crack with repeated washing, and the elastic at legs and waist can irritate the baby's skin. And because they don't allow moisture to evaporate, they can contribute to diaper rash.

It's worthwhile spending a few dollars more for good waterproof pants. A catalogue such as Baby Love Products (see Chapter 1) offers a choice of several with washable fabrics, Velcro fasteners, and soft leg bands. Nikki is a popular brand at $10 to $20 each.

Waterproof pants not only prevent leaks, but also (depending on how snugly they fit) hold the diaper in place without pins. If you want to avoid pins, consider tie-on diaper covers. Baby Snibbs are a vinyl tie-pant, 75¢ to $1 each, imported from Scandinavia, where they are used by nine out of ten mothers (or so the makers say). Many diaper services now carry them.

Biobottoms are a similar product, a diaper cover made from woven wool. And Diaperaps, knitted nylon and foam diaper covers, can be bought by mail order from Lamma Products, P.O. Box 3497, Granada Hills, California 91344. A set of six costs $23.50 U.S. and postage is extra.

If you're using diaper pins, stay away from those with plastic heads shaped like ducks or other animals. They can break easily into sharp pieces, leaving an exposed metal tip. To keep diaper pins sliding easily, poke them into a bar of soap when not in use. And don't hold open safety pins in your mouth while changing the baby. You can hurt yourself or harm the baby if one slips out.

Diaper liners are disposable inserts designed to keep a baby drier. After you fold the cloth diaper, place the liner inside, then pin the diaper. The liners can be used instead of double-diapering at night, for example.

Diaper Doublers can be used in either disposable or cloth diapers. Soft-Care Diaper Liners are used with cloth diapers only.

DIAPERING TOILETRIES

Cornstarch powder is recommended over talcum powder, which sometimes irritates a delicate skin. Johnson & Johnson now sells a cornstarch powder in a shaker container like their powder version. Neither powder nor lotions are necessary, however.

Never let your baby play with powders or ointments while you change him. The baby can inhale or swallow these substances and they can cause pneumonia.

Use mild soaps to wash your baby's bottom before putting on a clean diaper. You can then apply powder and a thin film of petroleum jelly or zinc ointment if you feel it's necessary. Put the powder in your hand first, instead of shaking the tin over your baby, in case he inhales some.

Johnson & Johnson is a powerful babycare tradition in many households, with its familiar powders, soaps, and shampoos. But at least one mother says she prefers Penaten products, because their scent is milder, less perfume-like.

If your baby develops a rash, stop using soap. Use only lukewarm water. Exposure to air is the most effective treatment for diaper rash. Leave the diaper off as much as possible. Plastic pants are an additional source of irritation.

Pre-moistened baby wipes are helpful when changing the baby, if you can get them to pop up one at a time. They're irritatingly unpredictable—sometimes you get only half a sheet, sometimes three or four together. You need both hands to pull them out of the dispenser and that leaves no hands to hold the baby.

Pre-moistened wipes are also expensive, and may contain drying agents such as alcohol, which can contribute to a rash. You're better off using them only for travelling, where they're handy in a pinch, and using tissues or napkins dipped into water or oil to clean the baby's bottom at home.

Here's a recipe for homemade baby wipes: Take a roll of

strong bathroom tissue, remove the cardboard tube core and place the roll in a covered container. Add a half-bottle of baby oil, pouring half of it on one end of the roll, then turning it over and pouring on the remaining oil. Pull out the centre of the roll and your supply of tear-off wipes is started.

TOILET-TRAINING AIDS

Your child probably won't be ready for toilet training until the age of about two. At that point you can buy a potty chair or seat adapter — a seat that fits onto the toilet — to help your child make the transition. Either product is efficient and is a matter of your child's personal preference. You can buy toilet-training equipment at specialty children's stores or department stores. Look for quality products made by Fisher-Price, Jolly Jumper and Babytyme.

A potty chair should be smoothly finished, with no sharp edges or splintering of any kind. The chamber pot section should be easy to remove. You may want a collapsible model. Some seats are adaptable and can be used on the floor or on the toilet with adjustable steps. Safety straps aren't necessary and may frighten your child, who might regard it as a form of confinement. Some parents like the plastic mini-toilets, with their no-nonsense design and their washability.

One potty seat comes complete with a music box that plays "How Dry I Am"; another only strikes up a tune when a child performs. A Jenny Lind training chair has a wood-like finish that makes it resemble a piece of prized furniture. It also has a tray and a security strap and folds for storage. An "adapter" seat on the market features a pony or duck squeaky top on the front.

These novelty items are no better than the no-frills versions. The brand you choose will depend on your budget and your tolerance for whimsy.

CHAPTER 6

Clothing

BABIES ONCE CAME in two ensembles: with terrycloth sleepers — or without terrycloth sleepers. But the era of the *haute
couture* baby has arrived. Even the wee ones are clad in
designer wear now. Your child can be dressed like a short
stockbroker, complete with starched shirt and a preppy bow
tie, or he can try on the mini-rock-star look of sequins, satin,
and studs.

Variety in babywear was sorely needed and the racks of
bold colours and cheerful patterns are welcome — it's a treat
to browse among the handpainted socks and Scandinavian
striped undies, the pastel jumpsuits and the handknit pull-
overs. Whether it's an Izod emblem or an animal appliqué,
children's wear has a fresh contemporary style that makes
shopping far more fun. But price tags can be absurdly high.
When a French cotton T-shirt fetches $30 or more, even the
most indulgent parent blinks in amazement.

Is clothing like this good value? Maybe not, but it's easy to
lose your heart to the occasional one-of-a-kind treasure for
your baby. Most parents, however, find that babies outgrow
their clothes too rapidly to justify paying so much for their
wardrobes. It's more economical to rely on hand-me-downs
and buy only the essentials. And as one mother says, "If I buy
a cheap brand of sleepers, my daughter's already too big for

them by the time they start to wear out. The poor quality isn't important to me. Paying more for a better brand doesn't make the sleepers fit her longer."

WHAT TO LOOK FOR

Make practicality and comfort your guidelines when you shop for baby. These necessities don't rule out style or fun. There is enough choice in today's babywear to satisfy all your needs.

Washability   Babies change clothing five or six times a day so washability is crucial.

Design   How functional is the garment? Does it allow easy diaper-changing? Infants hate clothing that must be pulled over the head. Look for easy front openings or wide-necked tops and T-shirts. Avoid buttons and other complicated fasteners. Keep it simple. (Velcro fasteners are quick and easy and can help the toddler to learn to dress himself.)

Clothing design should accommodate your child's movement. A baby is always active and his clothing shouldn't cramp his style. Elastics and tight knits are uncomfortable. Kimonos bunch up when he wriggles and kicks. A toddler likes a wide cut in overalls, for plenty of freedom. And loose clothing lasts longer than fitted styles. One-piece overalls and jumpers are preferable to separates as a child grows. Children's round tummies and undefined waists mean that they are always coming untucked from tops and bottoms.

Texture   Check the garment's fabric. Lightweight cottons and knits are absorbent and "breathe." Some parents insist on cotton clothing exclusively, but cotton nightwear is a fire hazard. Avoid hard seams and rough stitching.

Workmanship   Reinforced seams, double stitching, and strong elastic are all signs of sturdy construction.

Colour   Bold colours stimulate infants and delight the older child too. White stays white for about five-and-a-half seconds on baby and toddler both. Pastels tend to look faded

SNOWSUITS

No Canadian baby would be complete without a snowsuit. In autumn chills, January cold snaps, February slush, and March winds, the snowsuited baby is as much a part of the Canadian landscape as snow tires.

Here are some tips on buying a snowsuit for your child.

- One-piece snowsuits are easy to put on, and warmer.
- Two-piece suits are more versatile, won't be outgrown as fast.
- Snowsuits are sized like other children's clothing. Allow some room for growth, but if a snowsuit is far too big, your child won't be able to move easily. Beware of the stick-figure look.
- Check the snowsuit's outside fabric. Most snowsuits are 100 percent nylon but not all nylon is really waterproof. Synthetics like nylon are warm and wind resistant as well.
- Is the suit easy to put on and remove? Simple zippers, buckles, and Velcro fasteners are faster than buttons and loops.
- Is the stitching sturdy?
- Do cuffs fit snugly? Neck, wrists, waist, and ankles need to be well protected.
- Is the snowsuit's lining thick enough?
- Are knees and elbows reinforced? Twist and stretch the fabric.
- Is the snowsuit machine-washable?
- Look for metal eyelets, which prevent hood strings from tearing the suit's material.
- Are the suspenders on the suit's pants easy to adjust?
- Is the hood lined? Is it detachable?

quickly. Primary colours are a better choice. They stay bright and make baby easy to spot.

Versatility Adjustable straps, wide hems, and generous cuts mean garments can grow along with your child. Look for clothing that can do double duty too. Mix-and-match separates or reversible clothing stretch a child's wardrobe. Patterned undershirts can double as T-shirts.

Fit Sizing isn't standardized and size ranges in imported clothing are especially erratic. Weight and height are the best way to judge your child's size. And outdoor clothing should be large enough to fit over other clothes easily.

Flammability Avoid cotton and flannelette nightwear, especially loose, flowing nightgowns. These styles are dangerously flammable. More than half of the Canadian children who have been injured or killed because their clothing caught fire were wearing sleepwear when the accidents occurred. Canada has introduced tougher regulations on fire-resistant sleepwear. Cotton, polyester-cotton blends, acetate, and acrylic materials are not allowed, except in tight-fitting polo pyjamas and sleepers. Nylon and polyester aren't as flammable, in fact, they tend to melt, not burn. Tight jogging suits or polo pyjamas are the safest nightwear styles.

SHOES

A baby doesn't need shoes until he starts to walk. Until then, his Nike runners may look adorable but they are purely decorative. The adult shoe look-alikes can even interfere with his efforts to balance and learn to walk. Babies usually have fat flat feet. The barefoot baby is happiest, left to wiggle his toes in peace. Loose-fitting socks or booties are all he needs to keep his feet warm and safe.

Once he masters walking, it's time for the first pair of shoes. A flat Indian-style moccasin shoe is a good choice. This style is snug, supple, and will protect his feet without confining them. Sandals are also recommended. They let his feet breathe, and he can still wiggle his toes.

Should you choose a boot or a shoe for the new walker? There is some disagreement among experts. The high-cut boot is practical, but not because it offers ankle support. This style simply stays on a baby's foot better. The low-cut shoe is equally healthy.

After you buy the first set of shoes, check them every two or three months to see if it's time for a new pair. Stretched laces, stretched seams, or bulging near the top of the shoes are signs that your baby has outgrown them.

CHECKLIST

- Look for a trained staff when you go shopping for baby shoes. A self-service department may save you money but it's more important to make sure your child is fitted properly. Specialty stores provide a staff who can answer your questions and offer their expertise.
- The shoes your baby tries on should be bendable, cushioned, and thick-soled. Heels should be low.
- Have him take a trial stroll around the store in the shoes. When he stands, check the toes. There should be a half-inch of space around them.
- Does the heel fit snugly, but not too tight? Does it slip when your child walks?
- Check ankle height. Too low, the foot will slip out. Too high, it can cause blisters.
- Is the sole light, flexible, non-slip?
- Leather shoes "breathe." Canvas and nylon shoes don't.
- Don't buy secondhand shoes for your baby. Each foot is different and the shoes will be bent and stretched to the shape of the former wearer's foot.
- Running shoes are the only footwear your child needs after age two. A good pair of runners is flexible, and protective, offers adequate support, and is easy-care.

CHAPTER 7

Feeding

"I SWORE I'D BE DIFFERENT," sighs Joan, a thirty-three-year-old computer programmer. "Even before I got pregnant, I told myself that I'd never turn into one of those mothers who can talk nothing but baby, baby, baby. I knew lots of them and they bored me to tears.

"Two months after Carrie was born, there I was deep in discussion at an office party. And what was I talking about? Breastfeeding! I found myself talking breastfeeding with the same passion I used to save for politics . . ."

Breastfeeding is so fashionable now that parents planning to bottlefeed are sometimes treated like poor relations. Breastfeeding, deservedly, is enjoying renewed popularity, but the choice between breast- and bottlefeeding is personal and social pressures shouldn't make the decision for you. Formula-fed babies thrive too. Choose the method that suits you and your partner best.

In your baby's first months of life, breast milk or formula is all she needs.

BREASTFEEDING

Breastfeeding is the best way to feed your baby and the Canadian Pediatric Society backs this choice.

74

Breast milk is nutritionally almost perfect, is easy to digest, helps to prevent illness, infections, and allergies and promotes close loving contact between mother and child. No preparation of formula and bottles is necessary: breast milk is always available and is always the right temperature.

For the mother, breastfeeding has physical advantages. It encourages the uterus to contract and hastens its return to normal size after childbirth. It can speed up weight loss too, because it draws on the fat reserves accumulated during pregnancy. The breastfeeding mother also takes time to relax while she feeds her baby, a step that helps in her recovery from pregnancy and birth and continues to be therapeutic as she adjusts to a brand-new lifestyle.

According to Health and Welfare Canada, only one in four babies was breastfed in 1970. This figure had more than doubled by 1980. Now three out of four infants are breastfed.

Some hospitals are currently promoting breastfeeding the way they used to push bottles and formula. In maternity wards a mother who decides to bottlefeed may find that both nurses and doctors urge her to reconsider her decision.

The benefits of breastfeeding have already been outlined. But there are several aspects of the breastfeeding experience that are seldom anticipated. Here's what the books don't always tell you.

1. It's a full-time job, at least in the beginning.
Mother's milk is digested more rapidly and easily than formula. A breastfed baby needs to nurse every two to three hours, while a formula-fed baby can wait for four hours. When the bottle is finished, so is the feeding. But breastfed babies tend to suckle long after the milk stops flowing. The breast provides warmth, reassurance, comfort, and play. In the first two months, it's possible to be feeding the baby six hours out of every 24. (Most people only work 7½ hours.) You organize your day around the baby, not vice versa.

2. It's not free, although it is cheaper than bottlefeeding. The lactating mother needs a few basic supplies: a nursing

bra ($15 to $20), a nursing nightgown (about $15), and disposable nursing pads (15¢ each). You may also need special creams to soothe sore nipples. You need vitamins: for yourself, to replace the nutrients you give the baby, and for the baby, to provide the nutrients mother's milk doesn't have, specifically, vitamins A, C, D, and iron. Fluoride may be necessary too. You also need to add to your diet to make up for the calories you lose in the milk. But unless you shop extravagantly, the added expense will still cost you less than bottles and formula.

3. Breastfeeding in public isn't always easy.

You can give a baby a bottle in a restaurant or store and no one will object, but in North America you can't expect the same indifference when you nurse in public. Discretion can force you to retreat to less public places and therein lies a problem. Toilet cubicles are an unappetizing place for a baby to have a meal. Why don't more stores and restaurants provide comfortable armchairs for nursing mothers inside their rest rooms? A changing table nearby would also be appreciated. Department stores are starting to provide such facilities, but there are still too few.

Some mothers head for the nearest department store if they are shopping when the baby becomes hungry. The women's wear fitting rooms are comfortable spots to feed babies and as long as the store isn't busy, sales staff probably won't mind if you stay for 20 minutes or so.

Others brave the public eye and nurse in the open. They take a seat wherever they happen to be, wear clothing that allows them to breastfeed discreetly (a shawl or the baby's blanket are effective camouflage wear), and let the baby nurse away. Often no one even notices. As one experienced mother says, "A crying baby attracts a lot more attention than a happily nursing infant."

4. Only the mother can breastfeed.

The breastfeeding mother has to take on sole responsibility for feeding her child. Your partner can share other aspects of baby care but when your baby cries in hunger, you are the only one available who can satisfy her. This is a role some mothers cherish, but for others it's a problem and it's often the reason parents give for turning to bottlefeeding instead. Says one mother who chose breastfeeding but wasn't entirely sold: "In the first few weeks that the baby was home, I really resented the fact that every time the baby cried, my husband handed him to me to be fed. It was hard to tell if he was really hungry since we didn't know how much milk he was getting at each feeding. I had to spend most of my time nursing. I was tired and I didn't like that feeling of total responsibility."

Couples work out compromises, however. For the nightly feeding, the father may bring the baby to the mother in bed, then change her and put her back to bed after she is breastfed. Or the father gives a middle-of-the-night supplementary bottle to the child to allow mom to catch up on her rest.

The breastfeeding mother needs a solid support system, especially in the first few weeks. In hospital, get the advice of nursery staff on the right way to breastfeed. A good start can prevent the common difficulties that make breastfeeding uncomfortable: engorged breasts, cracked and sore nipples, or improper nursing techniques.

At home, a supportive spouse and family are essential until the new mother gains confidence. Your pediatrician or the public health nurse are additional resources. Many mothers have leaned on La Leche League, an international association that offers advice and assistance to breastfeeding mothers. The non-profit group is made up of enthusiastic mothers who have breastfed themselves.

La Leche League has acquired a reputation for fanaticism and you may find its motherhood-and-apple-pie dogma distasteful. But if you can overlook the ideology, you may find the League a source of practical, reassuring advice. Take the information you need and ignore the propaganda. In any case, on an individual basis not every La Leche League mem-

PCBs AND BREASTFEEDING

Can your breast milk be contaminated by PCBs?

Is it possible that while you nurse your baby, happy in the knowledge that you are providing her with "nature's perfect food," she is in fact taking in toxic chemicals?

PCBs — polychlorinated biphenyls — are the chemicals which contaminate soil, water, air, and food. Their use has been restricted in Canada since 1977 and banned since 1980.

Yet human milk has been found to contain PCBs. Their concentration is ten times higher in breast milk than in cow's milk. A Wisconsin study examined PCB levels in the breast milk of women who had been exposed to high amounts through eating contaminated fish from the Great Lakes. The researchers found that the PCB levels were high. But even more disturbing was their discovery that these levels dropped when the women nursed. This indicated that the PCBs were being transmitted to the infants directly.

So far the level of PCBs found in the average mother's milk is considered too low to pose a serious threat to breastfed North American infants. Research remains inconclusive but the benefits of breastfeeding still seem to outweigh the risks.

Canada's guidelines regarding safe levels of PCBs are a source of some controversy. The level currently is set at 50 micrograms per kilogram of milk. But a University of Guelph research team believes that amount is about five times too high. Their own research indicated that PCBs can become particularly concentrated in breast milk, a finding that the guideline does not recognize.

Breast milk contains about thirteen or fourteen major PCB components. Some of these are quite harmless, others can be very toxic. A level of 20 to 30 micrograms of

---

PCBs and Breastfeeding, cont'd.:

PCBs per kilogram of breast milk is not unusual, but 15 to 20 was the average amount found in a recent testing.

High-energy food like fruit, grains, dairy products, and meat are high in PCBs. Ten meals of fresh-water fish a year can double your intake of PCBs. Fresh-water fish are the chief sources of PCBs—bass, whitefish, trout, pike, carp, catfish, and pickerel. Ontario and British Columbia have particularly high levels. A woman who has been exposed to PCBs through industrial exposure or by eating large amounts of certain game fish may develop dangerous levels of PCBs in her breast milk. If her level is over 50 she will probably be advised to stop nursing.

How PCBs affect our health isn't clear yet. What is known, however, is that they are unavoidable. There are about 40,000 tonnes of PCBs in Canada. An Environment Canada study completed in 1985 found that Canadian children's diets expose them to far higher levels of toxic PCBs than the federal government considers safe. The average adult's daily intake of PCBs is near the maximum recommended.

No cases have been reported of health problems in breastfed infants as a result of low-level contamination. "Safe" and "dangerous" levels are not yet established. Even breast-milk testing methods have been questioned. So the hazards that breastfeeding *may* involve are not certain enough to discourage a breastfeeding mother. As one physician points out, the PCB issue needs to be kept in perspective. Cigarette smoke in the household, for instance, can pose a greater health problem to the infant; the exposure to carcinogens is probably higher.

If you are concerned about the level of PCBs in your breast milk, ask your doctor how to have your breast milk analysed or contact your local health department. In Ontario the Ministry of Agriculture provides a breast milk analysis free of charge.

ber waxes poetical over "the womanly art of breastfeeding" (as their book is titled), and not every representative of the League grows teary when she describes her nursing experiences. Unfortunately their literature has created an impression that has scared off mothers who might otherwise have learned from their expertise.

Local La Leche League chapters hold monthly meetings on breastfeeding which you can attend even before you have your baby; some groups welcome fathers as well. They also distribute a newsletter and other publications and provide telephone advice, a service many parents rely on. One mother recalls, "I don't think I could have continued breastfeeding Ian if I hadn't been able to phone the League leader and ask her how to handle my breastfeeding problems. She was always available and always encouraging. Sometimes it helped just to have someone listen and sympathize." This kind of moral support is important to an uncertain new mother. The discussion groups can also offer advice and you can meet other mothers at the same time.

Successful breastfeeding is the result of rest, relaxation, a good diet, frequent nursing, and persistence. Two myths exploded: breast size is not related to milk production; breastfeeding is not a form of birth control.

It's easy to convince yourself that your baby isn't getting enough milk when you can't measure how much she's taking. One indicator is the number of wet diapers you're changing. Six or more wet diapers daily mean that she's getting enough to eat (that is, if you're not giving her water too). And once breastfeeding is well established, twenty minutes of nursing per breast will provide the baby with enough milk and sufficient sucking time.

BREASTFEEDING AND THE WORKING MOTHER

Six weeks is a popular cut-off point for breastfeeding. When asked why, most mothers explain that they are preparing to head back to work so they want to wean their babies gradually.

But working doesn't have to halt breastfeeding. Consider continuing to breastfeed after you go back to work. You can opt to breastfeed exclusively or use both breast and bottle. The advantages?

- The close contact with your baby remains despite your absence.
- The chore of daily formula preparation is eliminated or at least reduced.
- Your baby may be less demanding if breastfeeding is continued.
- The daily transition between work and home can be bridged by the relaxed moments of nursing your child at the end of the work day.

Child care near your office makes breastfeeding easier. At workplace day care centres mothers take advantage of coffee breaks and lunch hours to nurse their babies. Having a nearby babysitter allows you to nurse at noon or perhaps at the beginning and end of each day. (Make sure your babysitter understands that you are anxious to breast-feed, so she doesn't feed the baby and hamper your own efforts.)

You can skip feedings too, but decide on the schedule ahead of time. Your milk production can adjust to fewer feedings but it should be done gradually. The baby needs time, too, to get used to a bottle. It's a rare baby who accepts sudden weaning gracefully.

Allow a period of adjustment of one week for every missed feeding. If you want to eliminate a mid-morning and a mid-afternoon feeding, for example, cut out only the mid-morning one the first week, and both feedings the next week.

Formula can be given for the feedings you miss (your milk supply will decrease accordingly) or you can supply your own breast milk. To do this you'll need to express your milk by hand or with the aid of a pump. The breast milk can be stored in the refrigerator or even frozen for up to a month. (If you have a chest freezer you can freeze breast milk for up to six months.)

It's the breast pumping that working women mention as the major inconvenience they experience. Finding a private spot to express milk on the job isn't always easy and the time you need to do it may be equally scarce. If you're forced to pump your milk while perched on a toilet in a cramped cubicle, your resolve may crumble. You might prefer that your baby rely on formula while you are at work, then nurse when you are at home for the early morning and/or night-time feeding. It's surprising how flexible milk supply is, changing to accommodate whatever arrangement you decide on. It may take a few days of discomfort — and a few leaps to the washroom to hand-express over-full breasts — but gradually your supply will make the transition.

Talk to your employer if you need to adjust your work schedule. Can you take time off every day to nurse your child or express your milk? You can offer to make the time up, and if your office has flexible hours this arrangement may be perfect.

Some women keep their plans to themselves and simply lock their office doors and pump their milk in private. If you don't have an office to retreat to, find out if you can borrow one or reserve some private space.

To estimate how much milk your baby will need, divide 30 ounces by the number of feedings your baby has every twenty-four hours. This figure is how much each bottle should contain. You will need to refrigerate your breast milk, another consideration when you are on the job. Some mothers feel self-conscious about storing their breast milk in the company fridge, alongside their colleagues' yogurt-and-cottage-cheese lunches.

Your working wardrobe should allow you to express your milk conveniently. Separates are easier than dresses, and patterned material can disguise accidental leaks. A nursing bra and breast pads are also recommended, and keep a sweater or jacket handy for real mishaps.

Even if you don't plan to save your milk, you will be expressing it periodically to ease the full feeling in your breasts. Don't express it for long periods, however, because it will stimulate your milk supply.

Pumping your breasts will take about twenty minutes once you know what you're doing. Express the milk into a clean container, then transfer it into sterilized bottles.

Frozen breast milk should be thawed at room temperature or in a bowl of warm water. Don't use your microwave oven for thawing. Once thawed, the milk should be used quickly because it is not as bacteria-resistant. Keep it in the refrigerator no longer than three or four hours. Breast milk should *never* be refrozen.

Antibodies are lost during freezing and your baby's system will not be able to absorb some of its nutrients. This isn't a concern if you are only using frozen breast milk occasionally. (By comparison, formula doesn't contain any antibodies.)

If your milk supply begins to suffer after you start back to work, take extra care. Improve your diet and snack on nutritious food like fruit and cheese. Try to rest often (as if that's possible with a job and a new baby!). Nap whenever you can and leave the housekeeping chores to your partner or hire cleaning help. Increase your nursing sessions, to encourage lactation.

It helps, too, to rely on supportive friends or ask advice from a local La Leche League group. Another breastfeeding working mother can be an important resource.

Ann, a Toronto radiologist, went back to work when her son Adam was five weeks old. She rented an electric breast pump from a medical supply store ("I couldn't use a manual pump") and twice a day she'd retreat to her office and pump her breast milk.

She emphasizes that it's important to have a reliable fridge and freezer at work to store the breast milk. "I froze a few days' worth of breast milk before I went back to work and I continued to freeze my milk every time I pumped it. I'd store it in freezer bags in the department's freezer, then take it home at night.

"The people I worked with had a good attitude about my breastfeeding. Nobody minded me using the freezer for the milk. I'd sometimes get interruptions in my office when I was trying to pump but generally everyone seemed to approve of what I was doing."

BREAST PUMPS

Electric breast pumps are the easiest way to pump your breasts. Unfortunately, most are also expensive — a thousand dollars or more. Their price tag restricts them to hospital use primarily. Breastfeeding support groups sometimes purchase one. They are also available for rental at a few dollars a day, theoretically, but finding one isn't unlike the search for the Holy Grail. Try a medical supply store. The monthly rental fee is about $35.

Gerber has introduced an inexpensive electric breast pump which sells for about $50. A battery-operated pump is also available now in the same price range.

The best hand pump, according to health professionals, is the Lloyd B, which sells for approximately $60 and can also be rented from medical supply outlets. It is lightweight and operates with a hand grip similar to a pistol.

Rubber bulb pumps—they look like bicycle horns—are widely available in drugstores, and they cost under $10. The bulb provides suction to assist in extracting the milk. In practice, however, these pumps are hard to use. They require a gentle, tugging action and the technique can be tricky.

Breast pumps based on piston and syringe suction are a more effective type. Monterey Laboratories sells the Infa Complete Breast Pump and Milk Storage System. The package provides a pump, adapters for different breast sizes, storage cylinders and freezer bags, twist ties, and labels for milk freezing. The cost is around $30 and you can find the product at Boots Drugstores. Evenflo makes a breast pump that allows you to express your milk directly into a storage bottle. The Deluxe Breast Pump Kit includes the pump, a plastic nurser, and an orthodontic nipple. Gerber has a similar kit.

Beware of breast pumps that don't work. Many mothers blame themselves when they can't pump their milk properly but often it's the pump's fault, not yours.

You can also hand-express your milk. The technique takes some practice but it works well and eliminates the need for pumps.

BOTTLEFEEDING

Bottlefeeding is second-best to breastfeeding, but it will provide plenty of nourishment for your baby's needs.

The bottlefed baby can be cared for by both partners, and this shared care is a distinct plus for the overworked new mother. Even if you're breastfeeding, it's worthwhile to bottlefeed occasionally so your baby willingly accepts a bottle when the breast isn't available. It can be reassuring, too, to know exactly how much milk your baby is drinking, something the breastfeeding mother often worries about.

FORMULA

Commercial formulas are patterned after breast milk. Essentially, formula is milk which is specially treated to be easily, completely digested. It contains basic nutrients — natural protein, fat from vegetable oils, and lactose — and is vitamin and mineral enriched. Some formulas are iron-fortified. Others are designed for the premature infant or the infant allergic to milk. In Canada controls are strict on infant formula standards so that nutritional needs are satisfied.

Ready-to-serve formula is the most convenient type available on the market. It comes in single-serving cans or larger ones. Pre-mixed formula is a good choice if you're uneasy about your water supply or if you are travelling. You may decide it's worth the extra expense to speed up the daily chore of bottle preparation. Concentrated formulas are more economical. Boiled water is added to each bottle in carefully measured amounts, one part water to one part formula. Powdered formula is cheapest but it involves the most preparation and thus the greatest risk of error.

Formula, like disposable diapers, is an ongoing expense for the new parent. You can buy popular formula brands like Similac, Enfalac, etc., at discount prices at drugstores, department stores and discount centres.

Cow's milk is not suitable for babies under six to nine months of age. Its sugars and proteins are difficult for infants to digest. Cow's milk can cause allergic reactions, anemia, intestinal bleeding, and diarrhea in infants. Skim milk and 2 percent milk should not be given to a child under a year of age. Low-fat milk doesn't provide the right combination of protein and fatty acids for a growing infant.

BOTTLEFEEDING EQUIPMENT

There are three types of bottles you can buy. Glass is the traditional baby bottle still used in most hospitals, but it's breakable. Plastic is much lighter and doesn't break, but it can be harder to clean than glass and may retain sour milk smells. Both glass and plastic bottles are recyclable, a one-time expense.

Clear plastic bottles are a better choice than opaque. Opaque plastic stains more easily too. And if you unwrap a novelty bottle among your baby gifts — shaped like a bunny or a bear, etc. — thank the giver warmly and resolve never to use it. It will be virtually impossible to clean.

Glass bottles can be sterilized in your dishwasher if it has a sterilizing cycle.

The newest bottle, the disposable nurser, has all the benefits of plastic and additional advantages of its own. It has a reusable plastic holder, but the actual milk container (a plastic bag that attaches to the nipple) is thrown out after each feeding. Playtex is one brand name for this feeding system.

Nursers are the most convenient type of bottle since there is no need for sterilization — the disposable plastic liners are pre-sterilized. You pay for this convenience (replacement bags cost 2 to 3 cents each), but the time saving may win out for you. Another benefit to the nurser is that the bags collapse as the baby drinks, so less air is taken in with the liquid. This makes the burping procedure less tiresome and supposedly cuts down on colic. Nurser sets have special nipples and you will probably have to stay with the same brand or they won't fit your bottle.

An ultra-modern Scandinavian baby bottle, the Maja, is now available in Canada. It's an anti-colic bottle with a valve system that allows air in while the baby sucks. The plastic bottle has a silicone nipple and can be ordered from Comfort International, P.O. Box 34184, Postal Station D, Vancouver, British Columbia, V6J 4N1.

Another new style in bottles is a type suitable for older babies. The plastic bottles, called Ansa, have a doughnut-shaped hole so an infant can hold them easily. "Designer" bottles are now available, made of polycarbonate plastic. While more expensive than traditional bottles, these newer models are stronger and won't develop the hairline cracks that cause discoloration. It may be worth it to you to spend a little more in order to avoid this problem. Totbots is one brand name and Infa-Grip is another.

Bottle nipples really matter, as any parent can testify who has tried to feed a frustrated infant with a bottle topped by a too-slow or too-fast nipple. Whatever kind comes with your bottles, make sure the milk comes out at a reasonable speed. (If the hole is too large, your baby will get too much milk too fast and cough and splutter.) And the nipple shouldn't go too far into the baby's mouth—it should only reach the roof of the mouth.

The Nuk nipple is recommended by many pediatricians because it's designed to be similar to the shape of a mother's breast during feeding. It collapses and expands easily and allows the baby to control the rate of the flow of the milk with less tongue-thrusting. The nipple fits all standard bottles and nursers.

Some nipples used to contain trace amounts of nitrosamines—chemicals created during the manufacturing process, which have been linked to cancer in animals. But in 1985, the Canadian government cut the permissible level of these chemicals to a very low level (10 micrograms of nitrosamines per kilogram of product), so this is no longer a concern.

Some manufacturers, however, are still exploiting the nitrosamine scare in their advertising. National Baby Formula Service Ltd., for example, says its Unisil silicone nipple is "the only safe nipple." Even more misleading is its claim that the federal health protection branch has detected "a high level of cancer-causing agents" in latex rubber nipples.

Silicone nipples are free of nitrosamines, but that's not the reason why you should buy them. They're much more durable than latex nipples, which must be thrown out after a few months. Silicone does not break down as easily, crack, discolour, or get sticky. The Pur nipple, made of the same type of silicone used to make valves in artificial hearts, is guaranteed to stay strong, soft, and clear for three years, and costs only slightly more than a latex nipple.

You may want to invest in a "baby bottle holder," once your baby is old enough that dropped bottles become a nuisance. These holders attach to the high chair, stroller, playpen, etc., so that the child can retrieve the bottle.

"Bottlenanny" is a Canadian invention, a bottleholder that can be used with any traditional bottle (but not the plastic nurser versions). Consisting of a plastic ring, nylon webbing and a plastic clasp, the "bottlenanny" doesn't pose a risk of strangulation and it's easy to attach. It's manufactured by Unique Baby Products, costs about $5 and can be found in department and specialty stores.

Another handy invention is a portable bottle warmer made by Snugli. No electricity or batteries are necessary, so it's ideal for warming a bottle in the car or while travelling or hiking. The bottle is stored in an insulated pouch and a heating pack warms the milk in ten to fifteen minutes. The pack has to be boiled before it is re-used.

Never put your baby to bed with a bottle, tempting as the idea may be. "Nursing bottle syndrome" is the tooth decay caused when sweet liquids like formula or juice are left in the mouth for long periods. It destroys the upper front teeth. It can also result when a baby is breastfed every hour or two all night long in the mother's bed.

BOTTLE-FEEDING SUPPLIES

- Six to eight bottles, with collars, caps, and covers (to prevent spillage when you travel)
- A dozen nipples
- A bottle brush and a nipple brush for cleaning
- A measuring cup with a spout
- A long-handled spoon for stirring the formula
- A bottle sterilizer, or a large pot or kettle with a tight-fitting lid and a rack (a tin pie plate with holes poked in it and turned upside down can substitute for a rack)
- Tongs for lifting hot bottles
- Several cans of liquid formula (always check the expiry date before using them)
  or
- A can of powdered formula, to which you add water

PACIFIERS

Pacifiers help calm an infant, but they work almost too well. Some babies become attached to them and can't give them up until they're two years old or more. At this point, the pacifier may disturb the alignment of their teeth.

Although there is no consensus among orthodontists about pacifiers, they generally acknowledge that an orthodontic pacifier such as the Nuk is preferable to thumbsucking. The nipple flattens when sucked and is less likely to put pressure on the baby's forming teeth. (You'll recognize the Nuk nipple because it's flattened on one side.)

Let your baby use the pacifier as much as she wants to in the first months. It's natural for her to need the comfort and sucking time the pacifier provides.

Pacifiers come under federal safety standards which ensure they are non-toxic, durable, and almost impossible to swallow. However, there is still a danger of improper use. Never tie the pacifier to your baby, her clothing, or crib. Babies have strangled when pacifier cords became entangled around their necks. And check them periodically, because a baby's teeth can bite through a worn pacifier, and she could choke on a piece of the nipple.

A new product, called the Soother Bib, solves the problem of lost pacifiers. The soother is attached to the bib with Velcro.

The latest in high-tech pacifiers is the Pacifier Plus, an orthodontic pacifier by Chicco Products that changes colour when a baby has a fever. It's distributed in Canada by Maltby Inc.

INTRODUCING SOLIDS

Take your time introducing solid food to your new baby. Your child's weight, activity, and appetite all influence her need for solids. In the first year milk provides almost all an infant needs nutritionally. Certainly you shouldn't start feeding solids before your infant is three or four months old, and six or seven months is the average age babies begin to signal an interest in food.

The more solids a baby is eating, the less appetite she has for milk, which is still the top priority in the early months. Talk to your doctor about an appropriate feeding schedule.

Cereal is the safest first food, preferably rice cereal. Single-grain cereals are least likely to trigger an allergy, which is the main problem solids can cause in a young baby.

Your baby's first efforts to eat may be quite comical, as the swallowing process is brand new. Keep spoonfuls small and don't force any food. The baby who turns up her nose at a particular food one day can be eager to try the same food the next.

Introduce one food at a time, always in small amounts. If your baby develops a rash or diarrhea in the days following a new food, she may be having an allergic reaction. It will be easier to identify the cause if you are introducing each item slowly.

Follow cereal with vegetables, fruit, and meat. By twelve months your child will probably be enjoying a variety of foods and dependence on breast or bottle will be waning.

Finger foods like raw carrot and celery sticks, wieners, and nuts should not be offered to the baby or toddler. They can cause choking. For a young baby, plain dried bread, teething biscuits, soft cooked carrots, bananas, or applesauce are good finger foods. Never offer your youngster a spoonful of peanut butter on its own; it can stick to the vocal cords.

You can make your own baby food with a minimum of effort. A food processor or blender can do the work, or you can buy a special babyfood grinder.

Food processors offer the most versatility, since you can blend foods finely for a young infant, coarsely for the older baby. But the babyfood blenders are sized for small amounts and they are easy to clean. If you buy one, check the blades for metal shavings. Running a piece of bread in the blender will remove these.

Commercial baby foods are the ultimate in convenience. Warm a jar, snap it open, and it's mealtime.

Not too long ago, babyfood manufacturers came under fire from consumers concerned about additives in the foods. The companies and the government paid attention to the criticism and as a result today's baby food is more wholesome. Heinz, for instance, the leading babyfood manufacturer in Canada, has no food colouring, salt, or artificial flavours in its baby foods. No sugar is added, except to a small number of fruits. Gerber baby foods have no artificial colours, flavours, or preservatives, though their "chunky" line of foods for toddlers are mildly seasoned. And some baby foods contain modified starches. Starches add calories and dilute nutrients.

Be a label-reader when you choose baby foods. Check the ingredients. They are listed in order of quantity. If water is first on the list, don't buy it, it's poor value. "Tapioca" means modified starch has been added. Make sure, too, that baby food jars don't show signs of breakage and that the vacuum-sealed lids haven't been tampered with.

Don't feed your baby directly from a jar of baby food unless she can finish the entire jar. The spoon will add her saliva to the jar and liquefy the remaining food.

Dried baby food is the latest twist to the baby food market. You add your own water. Nutritionally the dried baby food is the same as food in jars. The food is made with no salt, sugar, preservatives, or modified starch. It has the added advantage of cutting out waste, since you make only as much as the baby will eat. (This solves a common annoyance parents mention: a fridge filled with half-empty jars of baby food that eventually have to be thrown out.) The dried food needs no refrigeration and can be a practical choice for travelling. But make sure the water supply is safe.

Organically grown baby food is another recent entry to the market. Earth's Best Baby Food comes from the Green Mountains of Vermont and is available in Canadian health food stores. The gourmet line, which includes fruits, juices, vegetables and cereals, costs more than the mass-market varieties. But the emphasis is on quality, not economy, and the ingredients are all-natural. The products are grown, stored, and prepared without synthetic herbicides, pesticides, or chemicals.

MICROWAVE ALERT

Warming a baby's bottle in the microwave oven can be dangerous. It has caused scalding when it has been done improperly.

The oven does not alter the nutritional value of milk or formula when it heats a bottle, but it heats the milk unevenly. Different parts of the milk will be different temperatures.

Another important point is that the bottle may feel cool, but the contents can be too hot for the baby's mouth. At least one case of scalding has been reported, when a babysitter overheated a bottle of formula and her three-month-old charge suffered second- and third-degree burns to her mouth.

Use your microwave oven cautiously. Check the manual for instructions on heating bottles and baby food, or phone the manufacturer. The instructions should be followed carefully, because each brand of oven has different power levels and features. You'll have to experiment a little to know which timing and setting works.

It's worth remembering, by the way, that many doctors, including Dr. Spock, don't believe that warming a bottle is necessary. Babies often accept a cool or room-temperature bottle and its nutritional value remains the same.

The number one rule in using the microwave is to always

Microwave Alert, cont'd.:

stir, then test any baby food or milk before you give it to your infant. And remember, the container can be cool to the touch, but the food can be *very* hot.

Keep in mind that you only want to warm the food, not heat it. To avoid burning baby's mouth or tongue, always test a few drops of the milk on your wrist, or sample a spoonful of food to make sure it's warm, not hot.

Make it a rule that babysitters or anyone else who isn't used to your microwave oven cannot use it to heat baby's food. If the babysitter has warmed a full bowl of baby food, then reheats it after the baby has a few spoonfuls, she may not know that a partial bowl of baby food takes less time to heat than a full one. She may use the same time setting for both. The smaller amount of food will be far too hot and if it's not tested properly it could burn the baby's mouth.

Baby foods that contain a large amount of meat should not be microwaved in their jar. The droplets of water in these products heat faster by microwaves than the protein and fat particles and the water produces pockets of steam. The jar could break or the food could scald.

When you heat baby food, take the portion you need from the jar and transfer it to a shallow microwave-safe bowl. Heat it on a low to medium setting for less than 45 seconds. If you are not heating the entire contents of the jar, shorten the time accordingly—the contents of half a jar may only take 25 to 30 seconds, for instance. Test the food frequently until it reaches the feeding temperature you want. The time required will depend on the type of food.

To heat a glass or plastic bottle of formula, remove the cap and nipple. Heat at a medium setting until lukewarm. Let it stand for a minute or two, then shake the bottle to

Microwave Alert, cont'd.:

make sure the milk is at an even temperature. Test it on your wrist before you offer it to your baby.

For disposable nursing bottles, check the manufacturer's directions before using the microwave oven to heat them. Some aren't microwave-safe.

The size of the bottle, the initial temperature of the formula, and variability among microwave ovens all influence the length of heating time you'll need. Properly heated, the formula's nutritional quality will not be affected by microwaving. Don't overheat baby food or formula, because it could cause vitamin loss. And never use the microwave oven—or even the stove—to thaw frozen breast milk.

CHAPTER 8

Babyproofing

NEARLY EVERY MOTHER can recall a near-miss with her infant. The time he fell from the bed, or climbed out of his infant chair — or made a mad dash for freedom down the stairs you thought you'd blocked.

Babies become mobile so quickly that you may not even realize what your little one can do until he has already done it.

"Simon was eight months old and I'd put him in his walker. It was summertime so the front door was open. I turned away from him for a moment and the next thing I knew he had charged down the hall, out the front door and had fallen headlong down the concrete steps. We rushed him to hospital but he hadn't injured himself, by some miracle. I was absolutely stunned. I didn't know he could move so fast."

"Our daughter was sitting in her rocking infant chair on the kitchen table. Suddenly she sat bolt upright, overturning the chair and sending herself flying. She landed on the floor but luckily wasn't hurt — but my husband needed a stiff drink to calm himself down! We hadn't even realized that she was able to sit up on her own now."

You can't babyproof your home too early. (The ideal time to start is before your baby is born.) Most home accidents are preventable, yet Canada ranks third in young children's deaths due to home accidents. Two thousand Canadian children under the age of fifteen die each year in accidents ranging from swallowing a broken rattle to tumbling out a window. Accidents kill more children than the five leading fatal diseases combined. And in the U.S. three hundred infants die every month as a result of accidents.

From birth to six months the primary causes of accidents are burns, falls, toys, small sharp objects, smothering, and car travel. From seven to twelve months the causes are drowning, toys, kitchen accidents, poisons, strangulation, falls, burns, and dangerous objects. Somber statistics, but remember that the majority of these accidents could have been avoided. You can reduce the risks in your own household by taking a careful, commonsense approach to safety.

Babyproofing requires the instincts of a detective. Inspect every corner of your house and be on the alert for any potential dangers.

The most effective way to babyproof is to get down on your hands and knees and take a crawling tour of the house, room by room. This gives you a baby's eye view. (You'll probably prefer to conduct this particular tour at a time when you won't be interrupted! More than one mom mentions getting some rather peculiar reactions to her hands-and-knees inspection . . .)

Some homes, by the way, appear to defy childproofing. If yours falls into that category, you may be comforted by this mother's experience. Living in what she describes as "a ramshackle Victorian house," she was convinced her child—or the house—would meet with disaster, somewhere between the pedestal plantstand and the heavy oak staircase. Yet her one-year-old daughter has so far given the collectibles a wide berth and her parents have had to add only a few simple safety devices.

Babies vary wildly when it comes to the daredevil stunts that take years off the life of a panic-stricken parent. Your child may never go anywhere near the obvious danger spots.

Use common sense and your own knowledge of your infant to keep your house safe.

KITCHEN

- Keep a list of emergency phone numbers posted by the phone. It should include a poison control centre, your doctor's number, the hospital, the fire department, the general emergency number (911), your own address and phone number, and other essential numbers.

- Teach your baby early to stay away from the stove and oven, whether they are on or off.

- Get into the habit of turning handles of pots and pans towards the rear of the stove, so baby can't grab them. Use only the back burners whenever possible. Never leave a boiling pot unattended.

- If stove knobs are placed low on the front of the stove, remove them when you aren't using them.

- Keep safety latches on the fridge and all cupboards. Microwave ovens should be mounted, so a toddler cannot play with the controls.

- Don't let your child near an open dishwasher. The soap is poisonous.

- Keep small appliances unplugged when they are not in use. Keep cords short.

- Store household products — cleaners, detergents, disinfectants, etc. — in a high (locked) cupboard. Many are poisonous. Be sure all are clearly labelled. When you buy products like these, look for child-resistant packaging.

- Don't clean the kitchen wastepaper basket with poisonous spray. Your baby can inhale the fumes or get the spray on his hands.

- Wrap any sharp objects before discarding them, in case your baby manages to get into the garbage.

- Tie knots in thin plastic bags before discarding them, for the same reason.

- Don't store plastic bags where the baby can reach them.

- Never leave out knives or sharp-bladed utensils (like a Cuisinart blade). Store them in a locked cupboard.

- Place breakable items on high shelves.

- Avoid tablecloths and placemats. Babies love to grab and even a young infant can pull one down on himself.

- Get rid of throw rugs.

- Keep the baby or the toddler off a freshly washed floor. It can be too slippery.

- Store stepladder and stools out of reach.

- Make sure the dishwasher or the kitchen washing machine have safety locks.

- Put pets' bowls out of your child's reach.

- Keep your child's playpen at least two feet away from your work surfaces.

- Use only plastic cups and dishes for the baby — no breakables.

- Keep one drawer accessible to your infant. Leave it open and fill it with safe kitchen "toys" — wooden spoons, plastic cups, bowls and lids, brightly coloured plastic cookie cutters, etc. Keep changing the collection so your little one is always surprised and stays interested longer.

- Cover electrical outlets with safety plates or plastic plugs.

THE BATHROOM

- Keep all medicines and other harmful items (like cleaning products, razors, etc.) in a locked cabinet. Mark all medicines clearly. Make sure they have childproof caps.

- Use non-skid mats.

- Make sure glass panels in shower doors or bathtub enclosures are made of safety glass. (Houses built before 1974 did not have to meet safety standards.)

- Keep toilet lid closed.

- Lower your water heater temperature to 54°C (120°-130°F), to help prevent scalds.

- Place appliances away from water sources.

- Install heated towel rails out of your child's reach.

- Don't leave cosmetics or perfumes accessible.

LIVING ROOM, FAMILY ROOM AND BEDROOMS

- Banish bric-a-brac.

- Make sure bookshelves are sturdy enough to withstand a child's tugs. Wedge books in tightly.

- Place furniture in front of electrical outlets. Use safety plates or plastic covers to close off outlets from curious fingers.

- Check all furniture for sharp edges.

- Place all appliances—the TV, video equipment, stereo, etc.—out of reach but in a secure location. Disconnect them when they are not being used.

- Put a screen in front of your fireplace.

- Coffee tables send over 87,000 North American babies to hospital every year. Either store your coffee table or cushion its edges.

- Make sure carpeting is non-skid. If floor is uncarpeted, is it too slippery for an adventurous baby or toddler?

- Use wall-mounted lights instead of floor or table lamps.

- Choose curtains that don't hang within reach of a crawling infant. Make sure cords for window blinds or draperies hang out of reach too, to prevent strangling.

- Glass tables and bookshelves are a hazard. Put them away until your child is older.

- Antique furniture can be childproof if it's rugged. Some Canadiana is already well scratched and after surviving for a century or more it can handle a mere child's abuse with aplomb. But avoid lead-based paint, which can poison babies who chew on it.

THE NURSERY AND PLAYROOM

- Place crib away from windows, lamps and any electrical appliances.

- Use bumper pads in crib.

- Keep a nursery monitor in the baby's room, so that you can hear him from any room in your home.

- Don't use a crib made before 1974.

- Suspend mobiles well out of reach. Your baby could get caught in the strings.

- Never tie toys to the crib or playpen. The string could get wrapped around the neck and cause strangulation.

- Remove crib gyms and any toys that string across the crib when your child is old enough to sit or stand, to prevent possible strangulation.

- Check the baby's nursery equipment regularly in case it has been damaged. Are there any tears in the crib mattress or on the playpen pad? Are all bolts still secure?

- Remove large toys or stuffed animals from the crib once your child is learning to climb. He may use them as steps to help him clamber out.

- Check homemade toys for any potentially dangerous materials. Remove button eyes and felt mouths and noses; they could be torn off and swallowed. Make sure sewing is sturdy.

- Use wall-mounted lights.

- Make sure your child's toybox lid is safe. Could it slam down on his head or hands? Remove the lid or cushion the edges with foam. You can also install a "lid support," which allows the lid to close gradually.

- Remove the lock on a self-locking toybox. Your child could be trapped inside.

- Don't leave diapers soaking for a long period. Some babies have drowned by falling into diaper pails.

- Keep vaporizers out of baby's reach.

- If your child likes to rock all over the room in his crib, remove the wheels to ground him.

- Never hang a mirror near the crib.

- Store toiletries (powder, ointment, safety pins, soap) out of your baby's reach.

- Buy non-flammable nightwear for your baby. Canada has just tightened its safety standards for clothing; the U.S. has had tough rules for many years. Choose synthetics. Cotton and flannelette burn quickly.

OUTSIDE THE HOME

- Landscaped maintenance-free yards are great for city dwellers but can pose hazards for the curious toddler. He may want to sample a few wood chips or crushed stones, and interlocking brick surfaces can be rough on tender knees. Consider setting up a separate safe play area until your child is older.

- Check the safety of swings, slides, and jungle gyms in the neighbourhood playground or your own backyard. Does any equipment wobble? Rusty areas, sharp edges, or loose nuts, bolts, or clamps can cause injury. Are swings' ropes and chains in good condition? Is the playground surface soft? Sand is safer than asphalt or cement.

- Adventure playgrounds need a safety check too. Make sure yours is well maintained and designed for safety.

- Don't mow the lawn if baby is nearby. Flying stones or twigs may injure him.

- Make sure your yard is fenced in, with a reliable gate and a childproof lock.

- Inspect play areas for broken glass, sharp objects, and pet leavings.

- Cover outside electrical outlets.

- Never leave wading pools unsupervised. Drownings cause many home deaths and a child can drown in less than one inch of water. If you have a swimming pool, be extra-cautious. Teach your child to swim as soon as possible.

- Wooden decks can be treated with wood preservatives that are potentially dangerous to your crawling infant or toddler. The three hazardous ones — creosote, inorganic arsenic compounds, and pentachlorophenol — can be toxic. If you're building a deck, avoid these preservatives. If your deck is already treated with one, seal it with at least two coats of shellac or another sealant.

- Store shelves can be reached by toddlers. Make sure your child is constantly supervised, particularly in drugstores and grocery stores where items can be dangerous.

- Take elevators, not escalators, when you have a stroller or carriage with you. Escalators can catch wheels, cause accidents.

- When you visit other people's homes, make a quick safety check. Look for exposed electrical outlets, sharp-edged tables, breakables, open stairways, swinging doors, and medicines or cleaning products within reach. Are any windows accessible to your child? Bring along plastic safety caps for outlets.

- Be cautious when you take your child along to shop for groceries. Shopping carts are unsafe unless your child is properly secured in the seat. Take along a restraining belt or a harness. (In the U.S. a few supermarket chains have added seat belts to their carts and in Canada chains like Woodward's and Food City have joined them but they remain a tiny minority.) The Caretaker Seat Belt is one brand of belt you can buy in department stores or specialty stores. The Travel Safety Seat is sold by Consumers Distributing.

- Don't straddle your child's car seat across a shopping cart. The seat can be accidentally tipped by other shoppers or carts.

CHILD CARE TIPS

- Never leave your child alone on a changing table, in the tub, infant chair, infant swing or high chair, walker, or on your bed, the couch, or floor.

- Learn to ignore the phone. The telephone is the reason for many children's accidents. While a parent stops to chat, the child gets into trouble. Take your child with you or let it ring.

- Supervise your infant when he is in his walker and use it sparingly. Walkers are the single most common cause of head injuries in children under one year of age.

- Don't let your infant play with cornstarch or baby powder during diaper changes. He can breathe it in and choke.

- Avoid waterbeds. Cases have been reported of infant suffocation.

- Always keep the side raised on your baby's crib. You won't run the risk of forgetting to raise it before you leave him.

- Never go anywhere in your car unless your child is properly restrained in a safety car seat.

- Be cautious about teething foods. Raw carrots, celery, or chunks of wieners can cause choking.

- Never let your child run with sharp objects: lollipops, balloon sticks, pencils, etc.

- Take a first-aid course.

AROUND THE HOUSE

- Buy a fire extinguisher.

- Install smoke detectors.

- Stick decals on all sliding glass doors to prevent mishaps. Make sure your doors are made with safety glass.

- Place safety covers on all electrical outlets.

- Stick a "tot finder" decal on the outside of the nursery window. In an emergency, firefighters can locate your child's room quickly.

- Install safety gates on stairways (but avoid accordion-style gates in which a baby's head could be trapped).

- Get rid of poisonous house plants—or all your plants, if you're not sure which are toxic.

- Paint a red dot of nail polish on all hot water taps. Teach your child to stay away from them.

ACCIDENT PRIME TIME

Your household is more likely to have an accident if:

- ☐ your child is tired, ill or hungry
- ☐ your child is considered hyperactive
- ☐ the parent looking after the child is tired, ill, or overworked
- ☐ the child's environment is changed—new babysitter, vacation time, new house
- ☐ the household is disrupted by a new baby, visitors, a holiday
- ☐ parents have a tense relationship
- ☐ safety precautions haven't been followed
- ☐ baby equipment doesn't meet safety standards

BLACK SATURDAY

Saturday is the peak day of the week for accidents. Between three and six p.m. on Saturday is the worst time.

RUSH HOUR

Late afternoon is the favourite time for accidents. Parents are busy preparing dinner, baby is fussy, hungry, and tired and adults are rushed and impatient.

- Cover hot radiators with towels or block them off with furniture.

- Carpet stairways. Falls are a frequent cause of children's injuries. Carpets will help prevent slipping and will cushion a fall.

- Screen and bar all upper floor windows. Open all windows from the top when possible.

- Set your water heater at 54° C (130° F) or lower. A heater set at 66° C produces a third-degree burn in two seconds. At 54° it takes 30 seconds, an extra safety margin. Contact your utility company to find out how to lower it.

- Avoid space heaters.

- Avoid floor-level fans.

- Renovate with care when a baby's in the house. Today's paints are lead-free but before 1976 many contained unsafe levels of lead. The dust film you'll make by scraping old paint from walls could be toxic. Don't expose your child to this dust and make sure he doesn't eat any old-paint chips.

SAFETY DEVICES

No safety device can substitute for an alert parent. But they can help. You can find most of the following items in specialty stores or the infant's section of department stores. Mail order items are noted.

Safety Gates

Safety gates, which fit across a door or stairway to block access, are another way to protect a curious young explorer from harm. You can start using them as soon as the baby starts to creep and crawl (about six to eight months of age).

A safety gate can be more useful than a playpen because it is useful for a longer period of time.

Safety gates are mounted with hinges and screws, or they're held in place under pressure. Pressure gates are more convenient (you don't have to screw hardware into your doorjamb or wall), but they're not as secure as a more permanently attached gate. Pressure gates, which rely on the friction of rubber knobs against the wall, are simply not strong enough to prevent accidents.

Safety gates cost $20 to $40 and come in different heights and widths. Measure the door or staircase you want to block off before going out to buy one. Check for ornamentation, which could affect the fit of the gate. There are two kinds of pressure-mounted gates — one has a tension bar with one-centimetre (1/2-inch) gradations, the other is spring-loaded and has unlimited flexibility. For oddball widths, the second kind is preferable. Gerico makes the Gerry Swing-Open Security Gate, an expandable plastic gate with a variety of safety features.

Wooden accordion gates, similar in construction to wooden corrals, have fallen out of favour in the United States. In Canada, there is a voluntary ban, but the gates are still sold. They are dangerous because of their diamond-shaped openings, which can trap children's heads and lead to strangulation. Also, they are easy to climb, a factor to be considered as your baby grows. While recent models of accordion gates are made more safely, they have been overtaken by mesh, plastic, and vertical-slatted gates.

A popular safety gate with parents is the Supergate III. This is a swing-open gate that can be attached to wrought-iron railings — the only safety gate with this option right now.

Newly designed gates from Gerry and Fisher-Price make it easier to manoeuvre around them when your arms are filled with babies or other bundles. Instead of clambering over the gate or fumbling to unfasten it, you can release the lock by pressing a foot pedal (the Gerry Foot Hold model) or by using one hand to lock and unlock (the Fisher-Price Sure Grip Gate).

If you have stairs at home, install safety gates at both the top and the bottom. Since babies master the skill of going upstairs long before they learn how to come down, a gate at the bottom will protect your child from harm. (You might want to leave a couple of bottom stairs free so your baby can practise climbing safely.)

You can also buy a safety rail specially designed for the small child. The ToddleRail System is a handrail that is placed about 36 centimetres (14 inches) below the adult-sized version, so your child can grip it easily. Write to Toddle-Rail Systems Inc., 3191 Wolfedale Road, Mississauga, Ontario L5C 1V8.

Locks and Latches

Safety latches let you close cabinets or drawers to keep the baby out. You should be able to lock up the house for under $25, but you can spend more if you want a variety of gadgets. Playskool markets safety sets by room; they have a Baby Guard line for the bathroom and for the kitchen, with latches, door knob covers and so on, as well as a house set that includes a selection of safety devices for the entire home.

For drawers, you can buy long flexible plastic hooks which fit into catches. Cupboards can be closed with a slide lock. In each case, adults can easily release the latch but babies find it impossible. Most department stores offer childproofing locks. Hardware stores are another source.

Special refrigerator latches are available to keep the refrigerator out of bounds. You can also buy appliance latches for stoves, microwave ovens, and other appliances.

A homemade device that some parents resort to is a simple broom handle. Slide it through your cupboard door handles to close off cupboards to young hands. It's most practical for cupboards you don't need to open constantly.

A cord guard, manufactured by Playskool, prevents children from pulling over electrical appliances. The clamp is attached to furniture and can keep lamps or other items secured in place.

Safety Edges

Safety edges are soft plastic or rubber guards which round off sharp corners on coffee tables and other low furniture. An alternative is to buy foam tape from a hardware store and apply it yourself. Both Kindergard and Ikea sell ready-made versions.

Wall Outlet and Door Knob Covers

Blank electrical outlet plugs can be purchased at most hardware stores or children's stores. Local power companies sometimes offer them free of charge. Insert them in all unused outlets.

You can also buy outlet shields. These are protective covers that can be placed over outlets even when items are plugged in. PlugLock is one such product, made by Toronto's Robhill Industries.

Safety door knobs prevent a young child from opening doors. You can squeeze the knob hard enough to open it but your toddler can't. A homemade version: keep a sock over the door knob, held in place with a rubber band.

Fisher-Price and Gerry now have an electronic door alarm that senses when a door is opened and rings to alert parents. This reminds them to close the door or to intercept the child who might have set off the alarm. The Fisher-Price model is portable, making it convenient for a hotel room or for visiting friends and relatives.

Burn Protection

Developed in Calgary, the Stoveguard is a metal railing that fits around the stove top to prevent a child from reaching pots or burners. You may find this item in appliance stores or specialty shops for children's equipment. To order by mail, write to Staffordshire Marketing, R.R. #6, Barrie, Ontario L4M 5P5. Or contact Stoveguard, Box 188-143, 401 9th Avenue South West, Calgary, Alberta T2P 3K5. The device costs approximately $40.

The Sonmark Child Stove Protector is a similar product; it is also made in Canada. As well, you can purchase stove knob covers for gas and electric stoves.

Turning down your water heater to 54° C or lower is a cheap and easy way to cut down the risk of scalds. Another neat device is the Delta Scald-Guard. Pre-set at a maximum temperature, it also allows showers and faucets to turn on cold water before the hot water starts. This gives you a few seconds of grace to grab your toddler away in time. Try a plumbing store for this item, which is around $50.

Harnesses

Some parents hate the notion of a child harness, but they can be a real boon for active infants and toddlers at loose in the outside world. They allow a child to roam a bit but stay safe. They are also useful as a restraining belt for grocery carts, which are notoriously dangerous. (Shopping cart safety belts are also available now.) Mothercare-by-Post offers a harness with a stainless steel back clasp and adjustable waist and shoulder straps. You can find harnesses in retail stores too. Zip-a-Babe is one brand name.

A newer restraint is the Hand Holder (about $10), a bracelet which fits on the parent's wrist and the child's wrist, with a few feet of coiled wire between them. There are also electronic alarms that go off when a child strays beyond a certain distance, but these have not been popular with parents. The alarms don't sound until a child is some distance away, and they don't indicate the direction in which the child is headed. By the time the parent is alerted by the alarm, the baby or toddler may already be in trouble. The Nanny and the Toddler Minder are two examples of these devices.

CHAPTER 9

Health

FINDING A DOCTOR

You probably put time and energy into your search for the right doctor to deliver your baby. Finding a doctor to care for your newborn will require at least as much attention, if not more. Your relationship with this doctor will last longer and your role is far more demanding.

Your baby can't communicate so it's up to you to substitute. You need a physician who listens to your concerns, respects your attitudes, and treats you as a partner in the health care of your baby.

Start doctor-shopping before the baby is born. Ask your obstetrician to suggest a doctor, or ask other parents for their recommendations. Take note of their comments about their doctors too, since the type of bedside manner they like may not be appropriate for you. For example, a doctor whose short crisp explanations satisfy your equally matter-of-fact friend might not satisfy you. You may prefer a doctor who discusses medical matters with you in detail.

You can also contact local hospitals and request a list of staff pediatricians.

Your child's doctor doesn't have to be a pediatrician, however. A family physician can provide excellent care or you may decide to rely on the neighbourhood clinic. City hospitals sometimes offer a "family practice unit." This is a group of family practitioners, any one of whom will treat your child.

Armed with a few names, narrow the list to doctors who are close to your home and on the staff of a good hospital (preferably one that allows parents to room in if their child must be admitted). You will appreciate a convenient location if you find yourself making many last-minute trips to the doctor or if you have to consult him or her often in the first few months.

Set up appointments to meet each candidate. When you go, check out the office atmosphere. How friendly is the staff? How does the nurse handle phone calls? Is the waiting room designed for children? Are kids with contagious illnesses separated? How long are you kept waiting?

During your personal interview, ask the doctor a few questions about topics like breastfeeding, infant crying, or feeding solids. If you feel strongly about certain issues, discuss them now. You'll learn a lot about the doctor's approachability from the responses you hear.

If you plan to breastfeed, for instance, find out the doctor's view on it. A supportive pediatrician can help you make it through any rough periods, but a doctor who is unenthusiastic from the start will only discourage you.

If you are determined to postpone feeding solids to your infant as long as possible, make sure this doctor agrees with your decision. If not, why not? What is the pediatrician's policy regarding immunization? Is it compatible with yours?

"A parent may disagree with me on a few points," says Heather, a thirty-one-year-old Toronto pediatrician. "But once I explain my reasoning, we can usually reach a compromise." Dogmatic positions — on the part of the physician *or* the parent — can stand in the way of such friendly negotiation.

Review your medical history with the doctor, and your partner's too. Ask if the doctor is in a group practice. In a group practice of three or more doctors, at least one will be available or on call twenty-four hours a day. What happens when your own doctor isn't available? How do you reach him or her in an emergency?

What about over-the-phone advice? Some doctors have "call hours" when they answer non-emergency questions. How receptive is the doctor to parents' phone calls? What system does the staff use to handle them?

This introductory visit should tell you a lot. You'll know how knowledgeable the pediatrician seems, how carefully he or she listens to you, his or her childrearing philosophies and how well you can communicate with each other. You will have a rapport—or you won't.

Once you've found a pediatrician who has all the qualities you were after, don't overlook the last step. When you bring in your infant for the first check-up, make sure that the pediatrician demonstrates the same concern and sensitivity with your baby that you noticed earlier.

OFFICE VISITS

On your first visit with the baby, the pediatrician will take your family's health history, discuss the pregnancy and birth, and ask about the baby's eating habits and behaviour. The baby will have a physical examination and be given any necessary immunization.

If your pediatrician is on staff at a teaching hospital, the initial consultation will last roughly an hour, and later appointments about a half-hour. During these sessions your child may be seen by a number of health-care professionals.

Your child should have about four of these "well-baby" visits in the first six months; two in the second six months; two visits in the second year; and once a year after this.

At each session your baby will be physically examined and observed visually. You'll be asked about her behaviour, her feeding and digestion, bowel movements, sleep habits, and any problems.

Most parents find it helpful to prepare a written list of questions before they arrive in the doctor's office. Keep a notebook at home and record questions as you think of them. Write down symptoms, too, and take notes on the doctor's instructions. (It's so easy to forget what was said by the time you get back home.)

At all visits, bring along disposable diapers for your infant, an extra bottle, and any favourite toys.

WHEN TO CALL THE DOCTOR

Should I or shouldn't I? Every new parent worries about making unnecessary calls to the pediatrician.

If your baby is brand-new, call your doctor whenever you find yourself concerned. Doctors expect such calls from first-time parents (pediatricians spend nearly 30 percent of their practice time on the telephone), and you'll gradually learn when a call is necessary and when it's not.

"I ask my patients to phone me the same day they arrive home with the baby," says one pediatrician. "We set up the first appointment then and it gives them a chance to talk about any problems.

"If a parent calls my office, the nurse, who has had a lot of pediatric experience, can often answer their questions herself."

Eve, thirty-five and a first-time mother, finds her family physician tolerant of her phone calls. "Our doctor never makes me feel, 'Oh God, it's that crazy mother on the phone again,' " she says. "He's understanding and makes an effort to let us know that he thinks we are acting like normal parents." If your doctor's reaction is markedly different, you may want to reconsider your choice.

You're entitled to a courteous reception from your doctor, just as your doctor expects consideration from you. Try not to be over-casual about calling, and don't make evening calls when you could just as easily have called during the day.

Before you call, write down your observations about your baby's problem. Look up the number of your local pharmacy so you can provide it to the doctor immediately if a prescription is necessary. If you don't get through to your pediatrician right away and have to leave a message, leave your line free so that you can be reached.

Get your doctor's advice immediately if your baby:

- has an accident or suffers an injury
- develops breathing difficulties
- is vomiting
- cries for unusually long periods
- shows a marked change in behaviour: a sudden listlessness, for example
- suffers a head injury, particularly if there is vomiting or fever as well
- develops diarrhea (in combination with vomiting it can quickly lead to dehydration in young children)
- develops a high fever
- develops convulsions
- loses her appetite
- swallows any object

VITAMINS

Vitamin supplements for infants are almost as controversial as they are for adults.

A recent Canadian study of six-month-old infants in Toronto and Montreal found that nearly 80 percent of them were receiving vitamin drops containing vitamins A, C, and D. Yet some of these infants were already getting the same vitamins from commercial formula. The commercial formula alone already met their nutritional needs. An earlier study in Manitoba found that 33 percent of formula-fed infants were receiving daily vitamin preparations.

During early infancy, the breastfed baby needs a daily vitamin D supplement. Even though breast milk is vitamin-rich, its level of vitamin D is low. If the amount your baby gets is inadequate, rickets can develop and bone development can be impaired. So a pediatrician will usually prescribe a daily supplement of 400 I.U. of vitamin D until your child begins to drink vitamin-enriched milk. Extra iron and fluoride supplements may be necessary too.

Supplemental vitamins are not recommended with most commercially prepared formulas. These already contain the necessary vitamins. Fluoride supplements are recommended when the local water supply is low in fluorides. They are now available in drop form.

Vitamin drops containing vitamin D are highly concentrated and it's important to be cautious when you use them. Some droppers aren't calibrated and it is easy to make a mistake in dosage. A new brand, D-V: Sol, contains only vitamin D (many other brands include vitamins A and C and iron with the vitamin D) and has a calibrated dropper. Tri-Vi-Sol is another brand that is often recommended for the breastfed baby.

The recommended nutrient intake (RNI) for infants is 20 mg of vitamin C daily. Two ounces of vitaminized juice will provide the required amount. A baby shouldn't need a vitamin C supplement unless she is drinking only whole cow's milk, without also having juice or fruit rich in this vitamin.

Infant vitamin supplements are available over-the-counter, i.e., they can be purchased without a prescription. But they should not be given unless your doctor advises it. Babies are very sensitive to overdoses.

Ask your doctor if your baby needs a vitamin supplement. And when you give your infant vitamins, follow the dosage instructions to the letter to avoid the risk of overdose.

Vitamin drops are pleasantly flavoured, so your baby probably won't object to the taste. Squeeze the dropper into the side of her mouth. Squirting it towards the back of her throat could make her choke or gag.

When your baby starts to eat a varied diet, vitamin supplements are rarely necessary. Adults often regard vitamin pills as a form of "health insurance" and many doctors report that parents pressure them to recommend vitamins for their youngsters. But the Canadian Pediatric Society doesn't recommend vitamin supplements for children over the age of one.

In fact some medical studies maintain that overdoses on sweet, chewable vitamins pose more risk than the nutritional problems they are supposed to prevent.

Vitamin poisonings occur every year among Canadian children. The greatest danger to a child is the iron in multiple vitamins. Iron is toxic in even small concentrations.

You may find yourself anxious about your child's "picky" eating habits as she grows older. But she still may not need extra vitamins. Take a close look at her diet and you may be surprised by how many food groups she's including.

If you do decide she needs a supplement, be sure you store them safely. A handful of candy-flavoured multiple vitamins could send her to the emergency ward.

IMMUNIZATION

An immunization program is part of the pediatrician's care of your baby. Immunization against common contagious diseases starts at two months of age.

Measles, mumps, rubella (German measles), diphtheria, whooping cough, tetanus, and polio are the diseases children are inoculated against. (In the U.S. a tuberculin test is also included, at one year of age.) The first shot is the diphtheria, pertussis (whooping cough), tetanus vaccine (DPT), along with a dose of oral polio vaccine. This vaccination is repeated when a child is four months and six-months-old.

In the second year, the schedule recommended is an injection of MMR vaccine, which is a single shot that protects against measles, mumps, and rubella; later in the year another DPT and OPV "booster" shot. This booster is repeated before a child reaches the age of six, then again between the ages of fourteen and sixteen.

In the U.S., the measles shot is not recommended before the age of fifteen months, because the consensus there is that a child's antibody response is inadequate at one year and the shot would not be effective. But in Canada the current recommendation is to give the vaccination at one year.

Immunization has long been regarded as this century's medical miracle. Our generation rarely hears of diphtheria, the disease that once killed so many children. Polio has all but disappeared. Household quarantines for whooping cough or measles are dim memories. But disturbing publicity in the past few years has made a number of parents look at immunization suspiciously.

The vaccine that provoked the controversy is pertussis. Given in combination with the diphtheria and tetanus vaccines (the DPT-P shot), this vaccine protects against whooping cough. Infants younger than six months are most at risk from this illness, so protection starts early — at two months of age.

The whooping cough vaccine is produced by injecting dead virus (of the kind that causes the cough) into a child's body. The body then produces an antibody that makes the child immune to the disease. However, the virus contains toxic substances that can cause severe reactions in some children. Reports of serious reactions to the shot have begun to grow. Lawsuits against manufacturers of the vaccine have been launched by parents who believed that the vaccine had caused brain damage or other serious health complications in their children. A U.S. group, Dissatisfied Parents Together (DPT), lobbied to outlaw the use of DPT, and in Canada the Association for Vaccine Damaged Children has launched lawsuits against vaccine manufacturers.

In Ontario, a 1982 law that made vaccinations compulsory for school-aged children prompted the formation of the Committee Against Compulsory Vaccination. This group of about 400 concerned parents is committed to warning other parents about the side effects of immunization, including those related to the pertussis vaccine. They believe, for instance, that Sudden Infant Death Syndrome can result from vaccines.

In the wake of the negative publicity, all but one U.S. drug manufacturer stopped producing the vaccine. Britain had already seen a decline in the number of children vaccinated for whooping cough, after complications were first discovered in 1977.

The first Canadian lawsuit regarding the DPT-P vaccine came before Ontario's Supreme Court late in 1987. The parents of a nine-year-old boy sued Connaught Laboratories, the provincial government and two family doctors for $15 million in damages. The parents believe that the DPT-P vaccine caused their son's severe disabilities, which include blindness and brain damage. The family lost its lawsuit, however, and the ruling could block similar legal action by other parents. Nevertheless, a federal-provincial task force is studying the possibility of a vaccine damage compensation board.

The question of the vaccine's risks remains controversial. An Alberta study, released in 1988, found that since 1985 there have been increased reports of negative reactions to DPT-P after the fourth and fifth booster shots. (The fourth shot is given between fifteen and eighteen months of age; the fifth, between four and six years.)

While the report examined only "local" reactions to the vaccine — mild side effects seen at the site of the injection — which are considered annoying, not life-threatening, the Alberta study's results may lead to changes in the amount of vaccine that children receive, or the schedule for their immunizations.

Most doctors admit that some vaccines, among them pertussis, entail the risk of serious side effects such as permanent brain damage. But the disease the vaccine prevents is usually far more dangerous, while the number of children likely to develop vaccine-related complications is very low. One in 100,000 children suffers permanent brain damage because of whooping cough vaccine, for instance. The figure for the measles vaccine is one in a million and for polio one in five million.

Whooping cough itself can be fatal, however, and may result in death for one in every 250 babies with the disease. The risk of brain damage is about one in 2,000 cases. Other complications the disease can cause include pneumonia, encephalitis, lung damage, and seizures. Before the vaccination for whooping cough, the U.S. reported some 265,000 cases each year, and one out of thirty-three infants who caught whooping cough died from it. Statistics Canada counted over 1,129 cases of whooping cough in 1984. A recent federal study predicted that there would be two deaths in Canada due to the vaccine, but eighty deaths without it.

The medical profession generally maintains that the risks involved from the diseases far outweigh the risks of their vaccines. And they point to the fact that when the pertussis vaccine was not used in countries like Britain and Japan, epidemics of whooping cough resulted. Thirty children in Britain have died as a result. In the U.S. an epidemic was reported in 1983, in Oklahoma. And in Canada red measles have made a comeback. Outbreaks have occurred in three provinces, mostly among children who had not been immunized.

One important bonus to the controversy cannot be overestimated. It has alerted doctors to parents' concerns and made them more selective about administering the shots. Before the outcry, parents were told little about the side effects they could expect their infants to have after a vaccination.

Most reactions *are* mild. With the whooping cough vaccine, for example, they can include slight fever, prolonged crying, and fussiness. Your child may also develop soreness, redness, or swelling in the area where the injection was given.

You may decide that the question of immunizing your child is between you and your doctor. However, immunization is compulsory in Ontario and New Brunswick and throughout the United States. Children must show proof that they have been immunized before they are allowed to start school. (Exemption is allowed for medical or religious reasons.) Parents *can* refuse the pertussis (whooping cough) vaccine for their children if they decide it is unsafe.

Discuss the pros and cons of immunization with your pediatrician. Ask for a full explanation of the side effects you can expect your child to experience. Review your child's medical history. There are times when an inoculation should be delayed or even avoided. Fever, illness, a history of seizures or convulsions, or severe reactions to previous shots can lead to such a decision.

Children with allergies aren't considered to be at risk for side effects, though a severe allergy to eggs may rule out the measles or mumps vaccine (they are prepared in chick embryo cell cultures).

A new form of DPT and DPT-poliovaccines is being introduced now in Canada. These are injected into the muscle, whereas the previous vaccines were injected just beneath the skin. The new vaccines contain aluminum salts to improve the immune responses. Reactions are fewer and less severe.

With these new vaccines, children produce increased amounts of protective antibodies and boosters are only necessary after ten years, instead of five. The immunizing abilities are stronger. There are reports that Japanese drug manufacturers have produced a non-toxic pertussis vaccine, but it is not approved or available as yet in North America.

A vaccine for chicken pox is in the testing stages in the U.S. right now. Chicken pox is the last of the infectious diseases to resist a "cure."

And a meningitis vaccine has recently been approved by Health and Welfare Canada. Developed by Connaught Laboratories, the ProHIBit vaccine protects children as young as eighteen months against HIB meningitis. This disease strikes about 1,000 children under the age of five annually. It is believed to be the primary cause of acquired mental retardation. Eventually, the new vaccine may be approved for use on infants — the group most vulnerable to this form of meningitis.

MEDICAL RECORDS

It is awfully easy to lose track of your baby's immunization records. A few years pass, and you'll be turning the house upside down trying to find them at school registration time. Doctors will note each immunization in your baby's medical records. Ask your doctor to complete your own as well. Then keep the chart in a safe but accessible spot.

Ontario doctors are now providing parents with portable health records for their children. If your child needs emergency treatment from a doctor who doesn't know her, the medical information is right there.

Parents bring the record to each visit to the doctor to have it updated. It lists allergies, vaccinations, previous illnesses, chronic conditions, and other related information.

THE MEDICINE CABINET

Take a good look at your medicine cabinet. Is it a jumble of bottles and jars? Most of us hang on to an assortment of medication for years, barely remembering what they were prescribed for in the first place.

A new baby in the household is the best possible reason to clear out the medicine cabinet and start buying and storing drugs differently.

Like food, drugs spoil. If they are kept too long, they can become dangerous. Often there are no expiry dates to indicate when you should throw them away.

This is true of over-the-counter drugs, as well as prescribed medication. So it's better to buy in smaller amounts that will not grow stale. The small containers may not seem like the best buy, but the practice is far safer. And in the long run it *is* more economical; tossing out economy-size bottles of stale pills is an expensive habit.

Try to avoid stockpiling medicines. Most of us don't need them regularly, anyway. Buy them as you need them, in small quantities.

With a child in the family now, choose medication with child-resistant packaging. Studies show that safety caps can cut the number of child poisonings by half. No packaging can guarantee that it is childproof but the tougher a cap is to open, the better. Unit-dose packaging — in which each pill or capsule is separately packaged — helps to reduce the amount a child can swallow at any one time.

Drug manufacturers, under a new federal law, must offer child-resistant containers for certain over-the-counter drugs. This includes liquid medication like cough syrup. Not every size is available with safety packaging, since elderly people find safety caps hard to manage. But at least one size must include the safety feature.

Check your medicine cabinet every six months and get rid of any questionable items. Cloudy or discoloured liquids, broken capsules, dried-up ointments, and crumbling tablets are all danger signs. Ask your pharmacist about any medications you're unsure of.

The bathroom is not the place to keep medicine, even if you don't have children to worry about. The bathroom's warm, damp air helps hasten drug decay. Store all medicine in a locked cupboard or closet.

Poisoning is the top-ranking medical emergency among young children. Acetylsalicylic acid causes most accidental poisonings. But there are other familiar bathroom items you may not realize are poisonous. Mouthwash, for instance, can be lethal to a child. It has a high alcohol content, far higher than beer or wine. Its bright colour and sweet taste attract toddlers and the bottles are easy to open.

Start reading *all* labels, not just those on the obvious drugs and household products you know would harm your child.

Cosmetics and shaving lotions are potentially dangerous. Chewable vitamins are another hazard. Store them away from a child's reach.

Don't take medicine in the presence of your child. Children love to imitate. And when you give your child medication, avoid making a game of it.

Even over-the-counter medication you give your child can pose risks. Teething medicine, which is rubbed directly on the gums of teething infants, has caused poisoning when it has been given incorrectly. It's important to use this type of medication sparingly.

You may also be concerned about sugar in your child's medication. Sugar is added to make the medicine more palatable to infants and toddlers. Cough syrups, for example, are sweetened, as are most antibiotics. Ask your pediatrician to prescribe medications without high concentrations of sugar. Look carefully at over-the-counter drugs and check their sugar content. Poly-Vi-Sol vitamin drops have no sugar and neither do Vick's Medicated Cough Syrup (the lemon-flavoured type) or Robitussin Cough Syrup.

A FIRST-AID KIT

* Bottle of syrup of ipecac (to induce vomiting, *if instructed by poison control centre or physician*) * baby aspirin or equivalent (eg. Tempra liquid) * cotton balls * soap * roll of one-inch or two-inch cotton bandages * adhesive tape * sterile gauze pads * safety pins * tube of mild first-aid ointment * rubbing alcohol * calamine lotion * sunscreen * scissors * tweezers * thermometer (optional) * vaporizer (optional) * nasal aspirator (optional) * list of emergency phone numbers * first-aid guide

THERMOMETER

Rectal thermometers are usually used for infants but oral thermometers can be used to take an "armpit reading." Temperatures aren't taken by mouth until a child is six or seven years old.

You can also buy a heat-sensitive strip which is placed on a child's forehead and indicates a fever. It changes colour, reads F (for fever) or registers the actual temperature. This method, though quick and easy, isn't particularly accurate or reliable. It's not much better than your own hand.

A new pacifier called Pacifier Plus (by Chicco) changes colour to indicate a fever. A green dot suspended in glycerine turns black if a child is feverish. It's available in both Canada and the U.S.

Always shake the thermometer before you use it. To take your child's temperature using the armpit method, put the bulb of the thermometer (either rectal or oral) in the centre of her armpit and hold her arm securely against her side to keep it in place. Hold it in this position for two minutes.

If you are taking her temperature rectally, lay the baby on her back, lubricate the tip of the thermometer with a little vaseline or baby cream, and gently push the thermometer about an inch into the rectum. Hold her ankles to prevent her from kicking. Leave it in for at least a minute.

To read the thermometer, slowly rotate it until the black lines are visible. A normal temperature by rectum is 37.5° C (99.6° F). By the armpit method, a normal temperature is 36.7° C (97.6° F). You may find a digital thermometer preferable, because they are easy to read and sometimes faster than the conventional type.

Fevers don't have to be a cause for alarm. Doctors refer to "fever phobia," the parental panic that erupts when a child runs a temperature. A fever is just one indication of illness and isn't dangerous in itself. If a child has a fever over 39° C

(103° F), call your doctor. But children can be ill with no fever, or well with a high temperature.

VAPORIZERS

A vaporizer can be helpful when a child is bothered by colds. It adds moisture to the air and eases breathing.

There are two types on the market, the steam vaporizer (electrolytic) and the cool mist vaporizer. Both are effective. The cool-mist model, however, uses room-temperature water, making it a safer choice. A steam vaporizer generates steam through boiling water; if it is accidentally tipped over, it can cause burns.

Either type needs regular cleaning. (You can buy cleaning tablets at most drugstores.) The cool-mist type needs to be emptied of water and dried daily when it's in use. Otherwise bacteria multiplies and moulds can accumulate, since the water never boils. Wipe the container dry but let the blades air-dry.

Mineral deposits can build up on the metal elements of a steam vaporizer, so the inner cylinder requires an occasional scraping.

If you are buying a steam vaporizer, choose one with a low, wide base for extra stability. Look for one with a cover that locks on, so that if it is tipped it will leak slowly, not spill. Double-wall construction is another important feature. It keeps the water temperature lower.

Place the vaporizer at least four feet from the baby's crib and keep the cord out of the way. Don't move it while it's plugged in. And when you check on the baby, switch on a light. It's easy to knock over a vaporizer in a dark room. If your child is old enough to climb out of her crib, choose a cool-mist vaporizer. This type doesn't provide as much moisture but it's better for safety.

Hankscraft makes a full line of both vaporizers and humidifiers, as does Solaray.

CHAPTER 10

The Portable Baby

THERE IS NO SUCH THING as a quick exit when you are going out with the baby.

It demands plenty of planning (is he fed? is he in a good mood today?) and an armload or two of equipment. A minimum inventory: disposable diapers, wipes or tissues, a change of clothes, food, bottles, teething biscuits, plastic bags for wet diapers and dirty laundry, a blanket, a hat, and a sweater. No wonder new parents are intimidated at first.

Despite the military planning required, daily outings can save your sanity. Babies like fresh air and the stimulation of new sights and sounds. You may find that the baby who is fretful and cranky at home becomes angelic on the road. And for you, escaping the domestic routine can be a tonic. Whether you socialize, run errands, or simply take a long healthy walk, you'll benefit from the break. Your infant-centred world will open up a little.

There is a lot of equipment on the market for making the baby portable. This chapter will help you sort it out.

CHOOSING AN INFANT CAR SEAT

Your baby should be buckled for every ride in the car, including the first. It may seem heartless—and terribly unromantic — to surrender your new baby to the care of an impersonal, uncomfortable plastic chair. But facts clearly show that this is the safest way for him to travel, even on his first homeward journey. Make time to shop carefully for this baby essential. It's costly, so it's important to choose well. Even the type of car you drive can be a factor in your choice. Some car models can't accommodate certain makes of car seats.

Two kinds of car seats are available: infant-only and convertible. The tub-style seats, like the Infant Love Seat, are for infants. Convertible seats, like the Safe-T-Ryder, can be used for both infants and toddlers. (Each type is described in detail later in this chapter.) A new model by Evenflo (about $125), the Seven-Year Car Seat, fits infants, toddlers and children up to 27 kilograms (60 pounds) and 120 centimetres (4½ feet) tall when converted to a booster seat.

Research has shown that child restraints, if properly used, can reduce deaths by 90 percent and crippling injuries by 65 to 70 percent. Starting with Saskatchewan in 1980, all Canadian provinces now require their use.

But even with legislation, there's still a problem with parents who for some reason choose *not* to use the car seat one particular time. "It's just a short trip," they rationalize. "I'll drive slowly."

No matter how short a distance you have to travel, how carefully you drive, or how tightly you hold your beloved cargo, your child is at risk if unrestrained. An empty car seat is useless. Buy one that is convenient to use, and use it every day. A good rule to follow is: Everyone rides buckled up or the car doesn't start.

The baby who rides in a safety seat from birth is not likely to object to it later. For him, it's the only way to travel. Some hospitals now ask for proof you have a restraint system before discharging your newborn. They want to make the first ride a safe ride.

One word of advice: Practise fastening your baby into the car seat before you actually have to use it. Trying to figure out the seat's instructions when your newborn infant is already in the car and ready to go is a guaranteed way to increase everybody's stress levels. The day before you leave the hospital, give baby and car seat a trial run in the peace and quiet of your hospital room.

Keep your newborn centred in the car seat by tucking small baby blankets or rolled-up diapers between the sides of the seat and the baby's head. For $10, you can buy a baby's head-support, or "head hugger"—a ridged cotton pillow that keeps the baby's head upright in a too-big car seat or stroller. Totkins makes a washable "stuffer pad" (also $10) that cuts the car seat down to infant size. We don't advise using one.

Don't bundle your infant in blankets before putting him in the car seat. This makes it impossible to position the shoulder and crotch straps correctly. Tuck the blanket around the baby *after* the belt is buckled. And never place pillows or padding beneath the seat as this reduces its effectiveness in an accident.

For extra peace of mind on that first ride home, you or your partner should sit in the back seat with the baby. And you may want to discourage tailgating with a special "baby bumper sticker." Look for these in infant departments or specialty stores.

BACK SEAT FOR SAFETY

For maximum safety, the seat should be placed in a rear-facing position in the back seat. Infants always face the rear of the car, never the front, so their stronger backs can absorb the crash force in an accident. This position also reduces the risk of a whiplash injury and protects the infant from slamming against the dashboard.

The safest place in the car is the centre of the back seat. If your car is a four-seater, the back seat is still safer than the front. Avoid placing your child in the front seat unless you're alone in the car and must constantly turn around to check on him. When you must see the baby, put the restraint in the front seat, facing the rear.

The longer you keep your child in a rear-facing seat, the better. A baby should ride in one until he can sit up unaided and weighs at least 9 kilograms (20 pounds). Most parents wait eight or nine months before turning the chair around.

You can buy an infant-only restraint, or a convertible model that faces backward for an infant and then reverses to accommodate a toddler. We recommend starting with an infant-only restraint, then graduating to a toddler restraint later on.

INFANT-ONLY CAR SEATS

A tub-style infant car seat, which costs about $35 to $60, is lighter and more portable than a convertible model. It's easy to lift out of the car and doubles as an infant seat.

Should the baby fall asleep in the car, you can lift him out without waking him up if you use the tub-shaped model. Babies often doze off during a car ride, because the motion has a calming effect. (In fact, parents who can't get their infants to sleep sometimes resort in desperation to a midnight ride around the block.) It may be an important advantage to you to be able to unbuckle the car seat and leave your sleepy babe undisturbed.

Infant-only car seats are available through rental programs, if you decide you would prefer to rent instead of buy. Many rental services concentrate on this type of carrier exclusively.

The bucket-shaped Infant Love Seat, introduced by General Motors in the late sixties, is an excellent restraint, used in many rental programs. It's distributed by Dorel and sells for $50 to $60.

Unlike the Love Seat, restraints such as Evenflo's Dyn-O-Mite and Joy Rider, Collier-Keyworth's Cuddle Shuttle, and the Kanga Infant Car Seat are adjustable and have several positions. They're designed so they can be used in the house for sitting, eating or sleeping. However, not all the positions are safe for travelling. Always follow the manufacturer's instructions to choose the proper tilt.

CONVERTIBLE CAR SEATS

A convertible restraint costs $60 to $80 and, because it's quite heavy, usually stays in the car. The car's lap belt is threaded through the frame, and you don't have to undo the lap belt unless you move the restraint from one car to another. All you do is place the child in the harness.

With other seats such as the Infant Love Seat, you must follow two steps to secure the baby properly—place your child in the harness, and then buckle the lap belt around the car seat. If you make many short trips, you may find it a nuisance having to buckle and unbuckle the seat as well as the harness each time. A convertible seat with a thread-through installation may be better for you.

Dorel has the largest share of the market in convertible child restraints. The Montreal-based company makes a variety of car seats in the low-to-medium price range, all providing good basic protection. Evenflo is another excellent brand distributed by Little Darlings in Montreal. In the higher price range, Cosco is a manufacturer which is often a leader in safety innovations.

Convertible seats use several restraining systems. The five-point harness is the safest. It's belt-like and protects the shoulders, hips, and crotch. It also provides the most freedom for the child's arms and shoulders. But it's often misused because it takes so long to adjust the various belts.

The three-point harness with an abdominal shield is more convenient, since it takes only one easy motion to secure your child. Two shoulder straps fit into an armrest or T-shaped shield — the shield protects the hip area — and a crotch strap attaches to the underside of the shield. The shield also spreads the force of impact in a car accident over a wider area, causing less injury to vital organs. The state-of-the-art car seat is the Cosco Auto-Trac (about $160 to $180). It has a retractor system, similar to adult seatbelts in cars, that automatically adjusts the harness to fit the child. No harness length adjustments are needed.

Some convertible seats, like Strolee's Wee Care model, have both a five-point harness to protect the child and an armrest for comfort. If you buy one of these seats, never use the armrest without the five-point harness. It will not provide enough protection.

"Unless the manufacturer specifies that the armrest *is* a safety feature, the armrest is a cosmetic feature and will not protect the child in any way," says the Consumers' Association of Canada. "It is a very hazardous object for an unharnessed child to be thrown against."

The snug fit of the harness protects the baby's head (usually the heaviest part of the body) from crash forces. The closer the baby's head is to the back of the car seat, the less chance there is of the head going forward and then crashing back against the car seat.

Convertible child restraints always come with a tether strap — an extra anchor point for the seat when it faces forward. The tether strap reduces the child's forward head movement in an accident by restraining the top of the seat. It also offers protection in a side impact. The tether must be anchored to the car, which often requires drilling a hole in the rear window ledge, or the floor of the cargo area (in a hatchback or station wagon). Make sure an anchor plate is included when you buy the seat.

It isn't safe to hook the tether strap to any convenient hole or metal lip in the car. The anchorage *must* be bolted to the car's metal frame. If you're not handy with tools, ask your car dealer to help you install it. New regulations require all car makers to provide a pre-drilled anchor hole.

At one time, federal car seat regulations allowed manufacturers to design convertible car seats without a tether strap.

(Bo Peep introduced a tetherless model in 1984, followed by Dorel, Evenflo, and Strolee.) But while these retraints were more convenient, there were *not* as safe because they allowed more forward head movement. In a head-on collision at speeds above 48 kilometres (30 miles) per hour, the child's head would probably have hit the back of the front seat.

Recent government tests showed that some tetherless convertible seats did not meet the safety standards, and manufacturers started including tether straps again with their seats. Once your child is big enough to face forward, he should be in a properly tethered car seat, anchored to a sturdy part of the car frame. More and more auto makers are putting car seat anchors in their new models, but if your car doesn't have one, you can ask your car dealer or local mechanic to do it for you. It's an easy job and shouldn't cost more than $10 to $20.

BOOSTER SEATS

A booster seat is often the next step when your child outgrows his car seat. This cushion raises the child so he has a view out the window, and it also helps you to position the lap seat belt properly. You won't need to shop for one of these until your child is three years of age or older, and if your child is very tall, you may not need one at all.

Don't use an ordinary household booster seat in the car — they're unsafe. Choose one that meets federal safety standards. Booster seats reduce the risk of "submarining," caused when a child slips out from underneath the belt in a collision. Prices for boosters range from $20 to $45. One of the most popular models is Evenflo's Wings booster, about $45.

SHOPPING GUIDELINES

Whether you buy an infant-only car seat or a convertible restraint, make sure you can fit it into your car. Some child restraints simply can't be installed securely in certain cars. They may be too wide for the seat, or the lap belt may be too bulky to thread through properly. The rear seat belts in some cars require locking clips to stay taut and hold the car seat in place.

If possible, try out the seat in your car before you buy it. If it's a convertible model, place it in both forward and rear-facing positions. Try the restraint in both front and back seats. If the restraint has an armrest shield that swings up and back, your car may not have enough headroom to accommodate it.

Find a store with a wide variety of models so you can compare them. Practise adjusting the seat before you buy it.

Keep these questions in mind as you choose:

- Is the seat too bulky or heavy?
- Is it complicated to use?
- How quickly can you fasten the lap belt?
- Is the harness buckle easy to fasten and unfasten? Can a toddler unfasten it?
- Is the seat constructed with a single shell, or a double one?
- Is the material easy to clean? Washable removable covers are by far the most practical. Avoid Dorel's Velvet Touch vinyl, which doesn't wipe clean very well and develops bald spots over time.
- Is the harness easy to adjust?

The harness must be snug around the baby—you shouldn't be able to fit more than two fingers flat between the child's body and the harness. A loose harness is dangerous because the child can fly out. Since you will have to adjust the harness continually, both to accommodate the child's growth and his bulky winter clothes, make sure it's easy to adjust. Always use the chest clip which comes with the car seat at armpit level to keep the straps in place.

Bo Peep's Hi Rider is the most convenient to adjust. With most car seats, you have to remove the straps and thread them through another slot, a time-consuming and laborious process. The Hi Rider's design allows you to adjust the straps in a couple of seconds, simply by removing a bar at the back and then inserting it again.

Washability is important because car seats tend to collect cookie crumbs, milk spills, and other messes. Some restraints are made of vinyl, which is washable but sticky in hot weather. (Always check your car seat in summer's heat. A vinyl seat can burn your baby's skin.) Other car seats have a removable cloth pad which can be thrown in the washing machine.

If the car seat is not easy to clean, you may have to buy a washable cover for $15 to $20. You can also buy lambskin car seat covers. Another accessory to consider is a rubber mat which is placed under the seat and protects your car upholstery from the car seat's wear and tear. The best rubber mat is the Seat Saver, distributed by Jolly Jumper ($18 to $20).

SECONDHAND CAR SEATS

If you're buying a secondhand seat, buy a model that is still sold in the stores. Ask for the instructions. If there are none available, write to the manufacturer for them. (The manufacturer's address is usually on a label attached to the car seat.) Don't use a restraint made before 1983, when current safety rules came into effect.

Check a secondhand restraint for frayed webbing, cracks in the plastic shell, loose rivets, or loose stitching in the harness. The harness should be in good working order.

Has the secondhand car seat ever been in an accident? It may have worked beautifully but continued stress from the impact of an accident can weaken a car seat and reduce its protection value for your child.

If you buy a secondhand convertible car seat that requires a tether strap, make sure the strap is included, along with the

---

CAR SEATS AND THE CRANKY CHILD

A car seat may protect a baby, but that doesn't mean a baby has to like it! Infants often find them uncomfortable and make loud complaints. Here are some tips to help you cope with a baby who protests too much.

- Keep a parent in the back seat with the baby.
- Play story tapes or music.
- Offer small soft toys (but don't tie them to the seat — they could be hazardous). New toys keep him busy. You can buy toys specially made for car seats. They attach to the armrest shield.
- Avoid long trips.
- Dress the baby in comfortable clothing and an extra-absorbent diaper.
- Bring food and/or a bottle. The Bottle Nanny, a stand which attaches to the car seat, will keep the bottle close at hand.
- Make sure he isn't too warm. Several companies market a window shade that attaches to the car window with suction cups and protects the baby from the bright sun.

---

anchor plate you'll need to install it. If it's missing, write to the manufacturer or ask local stores if they stock spare ones for your model.

RENT OR BUY?

Car seats represent a big portion of baby-gear costs and rental is easier on the budget. There are Buckle-Up-Baby programs in many communities and the cost is minimal, usually $3 to $5 a month.

With a security deposit, you can arrange a short-term loan of a car seat (six to eight months). This deposit is refunded if the seat is returned in good condition. Assuming you get your

---

CAR SEAT RECALL

The Strolee GT 2000 convertible car seat is being recalled. One thousand units, shipped to Canada between March 1, 1988, and July 1, 1988, did not contain a tether strap, a Canadian statement of compliance label or instructions. The car seats were sold through Consumers Distributing and Toy City stores and should be returned. They will be replaced free of charge.

Cosco Inc. of Indiana has started a voluntary car seat repair program, covering Model 313 Safe and Easy, Model 323 Safe and Snug, and Model 423 Luxury Safe and Snug. About 320 seats were sold in Canada between January, 1984, and July, 1985. There have been reports from the U.S. about cracking. You can get a free repair kit by calling 1-800-265-9851.

The Fisher-Price car seat, Model 9100, is being investigated by the U.S. National Highway Traffic Safety Administration because of complaints. While this seat does not meet Canadian regulations and cannot be sold here, some people have bought them in the U.S. or received them as gifts. For a free modification kit, write to: Fisher-Price, Consumer Affairs, P.O. Box 16, East Aurora, N.Y. U.S.A. 14052.

---

deposit back, you will save at least half of the retail purchase price of a car seat by renting.

Lending programs are widely available. Contact your local hospital, a service club, a church group, a safety council, or a pediatric clinic. Some neighbourhood children's specialty shops offer lending programs.

If you decide to buy a car seat, you can sell it without any problem when your baby's outgrown it (they're always in demand). Or you can put it away for the next baby.

TEN COMMON CAR SEAT MISTAKES

All the child restraints on the Canadian market meet current government regulations and offer good protection when used correctly. However, many car seats are *not* used correctly. Three out of four children are at risk because their parents don't buckle them up properly. Here are some common mistakes.

- Not anchoring the tether strap on a car seat that faces forward. (The tether strap holds the top of the seat upright and prevents it from tipping forward in a sudden stop or crash.)
- Not fastening the harness firmly.
- Not using the automobile seat belt to secure the seat.
- Bundling a baby in blankets before placing him in the seat. (This makes proper belting impossible.)
- Facing a seat forward, when it should face the rear.
- Redesigning the seat. Instructions should be followed carefully and the seat and its restraints should not be altered even in minor ways.
- Tilting an adjustable seat incorrectly.
- Reclining a forward-facing seat. (They are safest when upright.)
- Not strapping the seat belts.

Keep the manufacturer's instructions handy for easy reference. Tuck them into the glove compartment or slide them into the car seat itself, between the upholstery and the frame.

Ideally, car seats should have a pocket to hold instructions. Manufacturers should also place warning labels on their car seats, clearly illustrating both the right and wrong ways to install and use the seat.

Ten Common Car Seat Mistakes, cont'd:

In a U.S. government study, parents were asked to select and use a car seat from among eight popular models. Only three parents kept the seats they originally chose.

This underlines the importance of understanding how a seat works, fits into your car, and rates in comfort for your child *before* you buy. If the seat is difficult to use, your child may not get the protection he needs.

Many stores and community groups rent car seats on a weekly or monthly basis. To avoid problems, consider short-term rental before buying. An excellent booklet on car seat use is *Keep Them Safe*, available free from Transport Canada, Road Safety and Motor Vehicle Regulation, Ottawa, Ontario K1A 0N5.

CARRIAGES AND STROLLERS

A carriage or stroller can buy you and your baby delicious freedom. With the right type, you can take your infant on long leisurely walks, shopping sprees and every kind of outing in any season. A stroller and a diaper bag are the only getaway tools you need.

After a car seat, this is your most important purchase. Your choice will depend on your lifestyle. (Some parents decide that for them, *two* strollers are a necessity: a sturdy style for Canadian winters, a lightweight umbrella-type for portability.)

Make your selection carefully, but don't postpone it. If you have a carriage or stroller on hand when you and the baby arrive home, you can start walking off your extra pregnancy pounds right away. Baby will enjoy the fresh air and soothing motion while you work out.

Years ago, newborns rode in boxy English prams. The stately pram was lovely for strolling in the park or along city streets. The high sides and hood protected a baby from sunshine and wind and the carriage's bounce could lull him to sleep. Dirt and exhaust fumes couldn't reach him, cold temperatures didn't penetrate.

Today, the old-fashioned baby carriage's popularity has faded. It's fast on its way to becoming a charming museum piece. Too large and too clumsy, it doesn't fit modern lifestyles. Parents want something they can fold easily into their cars and manoeuvre onto buses and subways. And no matter how regal the pram, price is a major obstacle — few can afford an accessory that costs $400 to $600 and is only useful for six months. As a status symbol, it has a brief life.

A baby carriage is worthwhile if you can borrow or rent one for the first few months, but there's no need to buy a new one. Manufacturers have introduced a new generation of high-tech strollers that include many of a carriage's advantages, but offer more versatility and at a lower cost.

Strollers are smaller, lighter, and more convenient than carriages, and best of all, they're collapsible. When you encounter a revolving door or a steep set of stairs, you can hold your child in one arm and the collapsed stroller in the other. For shopping and travel, a stroller is a better buy.

Until recently, however, strollers were flimsy and poorly designed. Federal safety standards were passed in 1985, after the government received complaints about strollers tipping, frames collapsing without warning, and brakes failing suddenly. Many parents maintained that their strollers simply did not stand up to daily wear and tear.

In a consumer test conducted in April, 1984, just before the federal safety standards came into effect, twenty-three strollers were studied. Only twelve met minimum safety requirements.

The new federal standards for strollers require reliable brakes and locking devices, seat belts and sturdy frames. Now you can be sure that even the lowest-priced strollers provide a margin of safety.

Strollers have also seen a revolution in design. Innovative makers like Italy's Perego and Japan's Aprica, in the higher price range ($150 to $400), have combined the comfort and styling of a carriage with the portability and compactness of a stroller—"sophisticated sports cars for babies," they have been christened.

Like a car, a stroller needs regular maintenance so you should look for a store that offers good service. Strollers get a lot of abuse—you bump them up and down stairs, hang heavy parcels from them, run them through rain and snow and sleet. Eventually the upholstery wears out, the frame rusts, the brakes deteriorate and you need help. A reputable retailer will stock spare parts and if necessary, go to bat for you with the manufacturer. A discount store may not even look at you after the first year of ownership.

The largest number of complaints about strollers have to do with sticking or jamming wheels. We recommend that you spray yours regularly with WD-40 oil. Any product with swivel wheels and so many pieces should be properly lubricated.

THE NEWBORN BABY

The fully reclining stroller is a must for the newborn baby. Babies sleep much of the time at first and they prefer a flat surface for sleeping, not an incline. If your stroller's backrest does not fold down flat, your infant may have trouble sleeping in it.

(Umbrella strollers generally do not recline completely. They are more suitable for a baby of three months or older.)

Another desirable feature for a stroller that will be used for a newborn is a reversible handle, which allows you to push the stroller forward or backwards. With the handle reversed, you can watch your baby when he sleeps and make eye contact when he's awake. In strollers without a reversible handle, all you can see is the back of the baby's head.

STROLLER CHECKLIST

Here are features to look for in a stroller:

☐ A handle that adjusts in height to suit both parents
☐ An adjustable footrest that can be lowered as the child grows
☐ A removable front bar or armrest
☐ Brakes on *both* back wheels, not just one (the brake should be easy to set with your foot, so you don't have to bend down)
☐ Shock absorbers
☐ Swivel wheels in front, and a locking mechanism to convert them to fixed wheels (for use on gravel paths, country roads)
☐ Double wheels in the front and/or back, which give added strength and stability and a smoother ride
☐ A strong, sturdy seat belt
☐ A seat that offers good back support and is wide enough to accommodate a child in a bulky snowsuit
☐ A self-standing feature that allows you to stand the stroller upright when it's collapsed (useful when you're loading it into the trunk of your car)
☐ A lightweight frame
☐ Easy-to-clean upholstery
☐ A canopy
☐ A wire basket for diaper bag or parcels (you can hang a bag on the handles of an umbrella stroller, but watch out — if you let go for a second, the bag's weight may tip the stroller)

This feature has a drawback, however. When the handle reverses, the stroller's swivel wheels are in the back instead of the front. They may be difficult to control and the rigid front wheels may be hard to manoeuvre in tight spots. Because of the awkwardness in steering, some retailers feel the reversible handle is more of a gimmick than an asset.

Perego has the Olympic Quattro ($270 to $330), a model that gives you the best of both worlds — a reversible handle and swivel wheels. When the handle is reversed, you can lock the front wheels (which are now in the back) and unlock the back wheels (which are now in the front). This double-lock system is very popular. Aprica has the Quartet, a similar model, and many companies have followed suit.

Also handy for newborns is a stroller canopy to provide sun and wind protection. Some strollers also have a boot to keep the baby's legs warm and dry in winter. (When not needed in summer, the boot can be used as a tote bag.) If the stroller does have a canopy, make sure it doesn't block your view of the child. Find out if it can be folded back or removed, or look for a clear plastic window through which you can watch your child.

BEFORE YOU BUY

A quality stroller will cost you $100 to $200 and up, but this is a worthwhile investment for shopping, recreation, or travel. Although children learn to walk after the first year, they usually need a stroller until they are three or four years old. A lower-priced model may not outlast one child, let alone two or three.

"I've gone through four strollers already," says Monica, whose daughter is now two years old. "If I were doing it again I'd buy an Aprica or a MacLaren stroller and an umbrella stroller too. I should have bought a good stroller to begin with."

When you shop for a stroller, open and close it several times to see how easily it collapses. Can you fold it with one hand while holding the baby with the other, or does it require two hands to set up and dismantle?

Take the stroller for a ride down the store's aisles. Is the handle high enough? If the handle is reversible, try it both ways. (Remember that a few inches in height are lost when the handle is reversed.) Does the stroller get in your way? Do you kick into it while you push? How easily does it turn corners?

Test the stability of the stroller by pressing down on the handle. It should be stable enough not to tip over backwards. Check for some form of shock absorption—the stroller should have plastic tires, not rubber ones, which wear down. Try steering it to see if it stays on a straight course. Examine the brakes, the seat belts, any locking devices.

If the stroller reclines for sleeping, are the sides high enough that there is no danger of the baby rolling out? Does the seat belt work in the reclining position? Can you fit an infant car seat into the stroller? (This is a useful feature. When your baby falls asleep in the car, you can transfer his car seat into the stroller without disturbing his rest.)

You may also want to buy a lightweight stroller for commuting or travelling. Some parents are disappointed with the standard strollers because they find them too heavy for daily use. Instead, they rely on a twenty-five-dollar umbrella stroller, which folds over your arm and is extremely convenient. Just don't expect it to last very long. You can use it exclusively, or as a back-up stroller.

Aprica is the Rolls-Royce of baby strollers, with deluxe models that cost up to $300. Styling is racing-car sleek, in colours like grey, burgundy, and navy blue. The Japanese manufacturer uses aluminum, a lightweight metal that doesn't rust, and strong square tubing. (Aprica commissioned designs for its Concor Mini model from the interior designer of the Concorde jet.) Strollers are definitely a fashion statement, as Aprica's success proves.

Rusting can plague strollers as well as cars. If you don't have room inside your home to store a stroller (as many city parents don't), you may need to keep it on the porch or balcony. The Canadian climate takes a toll on the stroller's metal frame, so Aprica's aluminum body is a feature you may need.

Perego, an Italian manufacturer, created the market for high-tech strollers and still has a reputation for quality. But its famous umbrella stroller, the Bye Bye, has been losing ground to those that recline fully. You can find it on sale these days at less than $100. If your baby is past the newborn stage, it's definitely worth buying.

Fully reclining strollers are now made by Alkot, Gendron, and Silvercrest. Other mid-price and fashionable brands are Pro Europa, Grand Caleche, Brio and Graco. MacLaren has an excellent umbrella stroller, light and tough, if your baby is beyond the reclining stage.

If you buy a secondhand stroller, make sure it's safe and stable. Signs of wear are easy to spot. If the fabric is torn or the tires run down, find a store that repairs strollers (there's usually one in every community) and ask them to try to salvage it for you.

If your secondhand (or new) stroller lacks accessories you want, you can always buy them. Add-on bags and baskets, weather shields, parasols, and washable seat covers are available separately. There are also handle extenders for umbrella strollers, to end stooping and backache. And don't forget a "head hugger" pillow, desirable in a stroller as well as a car seat, so the baby stays propped up when he's in a sitting position.

If you have two children close in age, you can buy a double stroller. Some twin strollers have side-by-side seats, which may be hard to manoeuvre through narrow doorways. Strolee and Jolly Jumper by Gerry make a piggyback stroller (about $200), in which one child rides behind another. (Only the front seat, however, has a back support.) In the higher price ranges ($300 to $400), there are deluxe double strollers by Perego, and Silver Cross.

Some parents put two children into a single baby carriage — the newborn lies down, while the toddler rides in an add-on seat. While convenient, this can be unsafe. Add-on seats were designed for older, metal-body prams; newer prams, made of wicker and plastic, may not be able to support the weight. An add-on seat can also unbalance a carriage—it should be attached to the middle of the body, not the very end.

In September and October of 1988, the federal government started buying and testing strollers and reviewing stroller regulations. This may be the prelude to voluntary industry standards, as with baby walkers.

BUYING A CARRIAGE

Carriages have distinct advantages, along with their obvious drawbacks. They are solid and comfortable. They have a more effective spring suspension system to cushion the ride and absorb bumps and knocks. In cold weather, they protect the baby from gusty winds. In hot weather, they can be covered with mosquito netting and used for naps outside on the porch or next to the pool. They are bulky, however, and your child will outgrow a carriage by six months of age.

Inside the house, a carriage can be used as a portable bed and wheeled from room to room. (You can often lull a fussy baby to sleep by rocking his carriage or rolling it back and forth.) Most carriages have a removable body which can be used as a bassinet, and some convert to a heavy-duty stroller. Mattawa's Three in One carriage (about $150) is a perennial bestseller.

Britain's Silver Cross is the showpiece of baby carriages. The styling is superb and the prices are outrageous. Its models start at $400 and climb to $800 or $900. A Silver Cross pram is a luxury and it looks it, every inch. (Don't confuse Silver Cross with Silvercrest, a Canadian company.) Perego also makes beautiful carriages, but is phasing them out.

If you're buying a carriage, new or secondhand, check

to see that it is the right height and weight for you. Is it collapsible and, if so, does it fit into your car? (Some carriages do not collapse at all.) Does the chassis lock securely onto the wheels? Is there a braking system for both front and back wheels?

Find out what is included and what is optional. Does it come with a mattress? Is there a harness or seat belt? (While strollers always have seat belts, few carriages do.) Is there an adjustable backrest so the baby can sit up? Storage space for bags and parcels? Is there a storm cover to protect the baby from wind, rain and cold?

A carriage may have small stroller-type wheels or oversized spoke wheels. Oversized wheels give a smoother ride, but if the carriage converts to a stroller, the smaller wheels that swivel are preferable. The best model has a set of swivel wheels that lock for carriage use and release for stroller use.

Carriages with larger wheels often have smaller interiors. (Appearances can be deceptive.) When comparing carriages, get out your measuring tape and find out exactly how much interior space they have.

If you are an antique buff, your search for a carriage might involve additional precautions. You may discover a wonderful Victorian-style wicker carriage, for example, at a flea market, an antique shop, perhaps in great-grandmother's attic. This is an irresistible find, but don't let nostalgia erase your safety concerns. How sturdy is it? Can an active baby tip it or fall out easily?

When buying a secondhand carriage, check the weld at the front wheels. This is an area that's exposed to great stress as you walk the carriage and can eventually come loose and break. If the weld isn't strong, don't buy the carriage.

TRAVEL BEDS

See Chapter 14.

BABY CARRIERS

Baby carriers are front or back packs in which you carry the baby. They are a brilliant invention. You can take your baby where a stroller or carriage can't go—hiking, sightseeing, down snowbound streets, or up steep hills—and all the while he snuggles next to you, warm, comfortable, and secure.

A soft front carrier wraps the baby around you, yet leaves your hands free. You can use it outdoors or wear it inside while you do household chores. Most important, it keeps you and your baby in close physical contact. The gentle motion, the warmth of your body, and the familiar sound of your heartbeat are soothing to your baby.

Fabric front-carriers tend to cut down a baby's fussy periods. A Montreal study of ninety-nine babies showed that of those who were carried in the pouches most cried an hour less each day at six weeks old—the peak crying age. "In Third World nations, babies are carried a great deal and crying is almost absent," said Dr. Urs Hunziker, a pediatrician at the Montreal Children's Hospital, when he reported his results.

For some parents, a baby carrier is absolutely indispensable in the first few months. Parents wear it two or three hours a day, every day, until their backs and shoulders can't take the strain any more. They go to parties, see films, dine out in restaurants, cook at home, all with the baby strapped to their chests. To their infants, their carriers are instant tranquillizers.

"We really liked our Snugli when Jonathan was a young infant," says Boyd, 36. "When he was bigger the Baby Matey was better for him. Both carriers were essentials. They would quiet him when he was cranky and even if he protested when we put him in, he would settle down quickly. Debbie and I took him with us to a movie when he was just a few weeks old and he slept for two hours on my chest."

Backpacks are equally popular, but a baby should not be carried on your back until he can hold his head up without support (about 16 to 20 weeks old). Until then, his neck isn't strong enough to withstand jolts and he could suffer a neck injury.

You can carry your child up front until he is four or five months old, and on your back until he's two-and-a-half to three years old, depending on your stamina — and his weight.

The main disadvantage of baby carriers is that *you* are the means of locomotion. Even the best-fitting carrier can become uncomfortable, particularly with older, heavier children. Bending over is tricky and can be hazardous if the baby is not tied in securely. And that extra weight at chest or shoulder level throws off your balance and can result in falls if you slip.

Keeping the baby warm on winter outings — particularly those dangling arms and legs — can pose a problem. Keeping yourself warm is also a challenge. Does the carrier go under your coat or over it? If you wear it over your coat, can you remove the coat without disturbing the baby? It's usually a matter of trial and error.

There doesn't seem to be a painless way to bundle and unbundle a baby in his carrier. Canada's climate means winter snowsuits and bulky clothing adds to the struggle.

Be sure you will feel comfortable wearing a baby carrier before you invest in one. Some parents find the baby's weight too heavy around their necks or shoulders. If you do want one, decide whether you prefer a front pack, a backpack, or a convertible pack (a soft fabric carrier that can be worn in either the front or back position).

A final decision concerns the type of fabric to buy. While originally made of heavy corduroy, baby carriers now come in more lightweight fabrics such as denim, chambray, seersucker, and cotton mesh. If you have a winter baby, a warm fabric like denim or corduroy is best. For a summer baby, choose a cool, lightweight cotton like seersucker.

Snugli is the best-known brand of baby carrier, made by

Snugli Canada Ltd. of Vancouver and sold in Canada since 1968. It has a double-pouch design. The baby is placed in the inner pouch, and the outer one is zipped over it for extra warmth and support. It can be worn as a front or back carrier, with tucks in the pouches that can be let out as the baby grows and taken in later to accommodate another newborn. Cost is about $45.

Though the Snugli can be worn as a back carrier when the baby gets older, you may find it doesn't offer enough support for you to carry the baby comfortably. A back pack with a metal frame is preferable, especially for winter use. Another drawback to the Snugli is that it doesn't provide enough head support for a newborn. You need to cradle the baby's head with one hand.

The Gerry Cuddlepack is a similar pouch-style cloth carrier in the same price range ($40 to $50). It offers more head support than the Snugli — there is a foam headrest for added neck support — and can be used for breastfeeding. A zipper on the inner pouch makes it possible for your baby to nurse while you hold him.

A newer carrier is the Baby Matey, made by Rondo Sales in Toronto ($37 to $45). Modelled after an ancient Oriental carrier, it can be worn on the chest, back, or hip, or as a nursing sling. Its six straps, which wrap around the waist, shoulders, and back, distribute the baby's weight more evenly, making it comfortable to use. Many parents prefer the Baby Matey to the Snugli.

In a 1984 consumer test of nine baby carriers the Baby Matey was voted the most comfortable, versatile and durable. Not everyone liked it, however. Many testers found the instructions confusing and had trouble fitting the carrier properly.

A new carrier that is finding favour with a lot of parents is the Evenflo Napsack. It's more expensive than most (about $60), but has more convenient zip-up pouches for carrying baby and accessories too.

CARRIER CHECKLIST

When buying a soft front carrier, try it on first. Use a doll if your baby hasn't been born yet. Here are some points to check, most of which apply to frame carriers too.

- Does the carrier provide enough head and neck support for the baby and allow you full use of both hands? Is the head support adjustable? Is it detachable?
- Are the shoulder straps wide and well padded? Are they long enough to fit both parents? Is there a waist strap to take some of the strain off your shoulders?
- Are the materials sturdy, the stitching strong? (Weight-bearing sewn parts should be double-stitched or reinforced for added strength.)
- Are the snaps, zippers, and buckles secure?
- Are the leg openings large enough to accommodate bulky winter clothing? They shouldn't cut off the baby's circulation or chafe his legs. If possible, they should have padding for added comfort.
- Is the fabric suitable for the seasons in which you will be wearing it?
- Is the fabric washable? Is there a removable bib for laundering?
- Can baby face back and front? (The reverse position should never be used before a baby can hold up his head.)
- Are the clasps easy to open and close, preferably with one hand, leaving the other free to hold the baby?

Look for a carrier that is easy to put on and remove without outside help. Practise on a doll before trying it with your infant.

When you carry the baby in the pack, remember to bend from the knees when you lean over or stoop, instead

Carrier Checklist, cont'd:

of bending from the waist. This reduces the risk of the baby toppling out head first.

Never use a carrier in a car, even with the seat belt strapped around both of you. The only safe way for a baby to travel by car is in an approved car seat.

Don't bicycle with your baby in the carrier. The carrier throws off your centre of gravity and if you fall, there is no way you can protect your child.

New mothers often take post-natal fitness classes with their infants strapped to their chests, but more active sports can be dangerous. The extra weight can make you lose your balance. Skiing, skating, and bicycling aren't recommended.

CHAPTER 11

Stepping Out

BABYSITTERS ARE THE new parent's salvation. They return to the parent a gift that has been temporarily stolen from them— time for themselves. Even the most loving and devoted par- ents sometimes need to get away from the baby. Don't feel guilty. It's reasonable to want to take an occasional break from any responsibility, including infant care.

Though it can be a lot of work lining up reliable baby sitters, it's essential to do it—essential to your relationship. You and your partner have to get to know each other again as a couple, free from your new-found roles as parents.

It's normal to be nervous the first few times you have a sitter. It may take several outings before you feel comfortable and stop fretting about the baby. But soldier on. It's worth it, for you and for the baby.

The first few times you fly solo, leave the baby with a loving trustworthy caregiver—a grandparent or close friend is ideal—and call home often, whenever you feel the need. Stay away as long as you feel comfortable and do something you really enjoy.

Once you see how delightful it is to escape, even for a couple of hours, you will want to expand your babysitting resources beyond your immediate family and friends. Most parents have a roster of at least three or four reliable sitters they can call at short notice. Some find a teenager who is willing to sit every Saturday night and pay her whether they go out or not.

Saturday nights are the busiest times for babysitters. Unless you call early in the week, you may find the best sitters are already booked up. Too many rejections and you start to wonder whether it's really necessary to go out at all. The movie line-ups are longer on Saturday nights, the restaurants more crowded, the parties noisier and more hectic.

Consider using a sitter for times other than weekends. Some regular time free of the baby during the week is a boon to a mother's sanity and a couple's relationship. If you don't feel like leaving home, ask the sitter to take the baby for a long walk while you nap, read, bathe, finish some work, or just relax.

Finding good babysitters is often a problem. Demand is greater than supply in most communities and turnover is constant. Other parents may be reluctant to give out names, hoping to keep their treasures to themselves. With so much competition, how can you get an edge?

In this chapter, we'll tell you where to look for babysitters and how to screen them so they meet your needs. And since finding the right person is only half the battle, we'll show you how to prepare the babysitter for illness, emergencies, and unexpected situations that may crop up in your absence.

FINDING A BABYSITTER

Before starting your search, you should know what you're looking for. Do you want a teenager or a mature adult? Do you want someone to hold the fort while your child sleeps, or someone who can bathe, feed, and play with the baby while she's awake? Once you sort out your preferences, you'll have an easier time finding the right babysitter.

Teenagers are readily available and not expensive, but you

may be nervous about leaving your newborn with one. Try to find a sitter who has training, experience, and a mother living nearby who can give help or advice if you can't be reached.

To find a babysitter, ask your friends and neighbours if they have or know any teenagers who babysit. Ask if the teenagers have taken any babysitting courses such as those offered by St. John Ambulance, the Canadian Red Cross or local parks and recreation departments, and if they have cared for younger brothers and sisters while their parents were away.

Check bulletin boards in your local supermarkets, community centres, schools, day care centres, YW/YMCAs, churches, or libraries, and post your own notices at the same time. If you live near a college, university, school of education, or nursing school, check with the student employment office and the foreign students' centre, if there is one.

What's the minimum age for babysitting? Fourteen years old is the age at which most teenagers start babysitting. The great advantage of younger teens is their availability. Once they turn 16, their own social life starts. A party, a date, or a dance will win out over a babysitting job every time.

For daytime babysitting, when your baby is awake and active, you may prefer a more mature babysitter. There are women in local neighbourhoods, probably yours too, already caring for their own preschool children or grandchildren in their homes. They welcome a little extra money along with companionship for their own charges.

Senior citizens, especially those who are separated from their own grandchildren, often love to babysit. Check with local churches, senior citizens' groups, and retirement homes, but be sure the person you pick is active, energetic, and in good health. Carrying a heavy baby or chasing after a toddler can be too much for some older people, no matter how willing they are.

If you can't find a babysitter through word of mouth and informal sources, scan the classified advertisements in local newspapers or run your own ad. Advertising is a great way to build up a roster of babysitters or to find someone to sit regularly every weekend, but be prepared for lots of calls and the need for tough screening.

Your child's aunts and uncles can be marvellous sitters. If you take their children, say for a long weekend once a year, they'll do the same for you. Or you can trade off with another parent on a regular basis. It's certainly tiring taking care of more than one baby, but you'll probably find it's worth it when it's your turn to be off.

A disadvantage to using other parents with children is the risk of either your child or theirs becoming ill. But if you must go out when your child is sick, a friend who also has a sick child can save the day. Bundle up your child and take her over.

As a last resort, you can use a babysitting agency. Agency sitters are more expensive — $3.50 to $5 an hour — since you must pay the agency as well as the sitter. There's usually a minimum of four hours at night, five hours during the day, plus a transportation fee. For names of agencies, ask other parents or check the yellow pages of your telephone directory. Find out if the agency sends a different sitter each time you make a request, or if you can get your favourite one again and again. Agency sitters are screened and they have experience, but this doesn't guarantee you'll be impressed by each one sent to you.

The main advantage of an agency is that they come through in the crunch. If you have a lot of parties at Christmas and New Year's, a busy time for sitters, an agency can usually find you someone when all your regular sitters are booked up.

HOW TO HIRE A SITTER

You probably won't have enough time to interview everyone who wants to babysit for you, so use the telephone to screen applicants. Ask for vital statistics — name, address, phone number, and a brief summary of their experience — and listen

PLAY GROUPS AND CO-OPS

Play groups offer sociable times for both parent and child. Most neighbourhoods have a few to choose from. Or, when you have made a few friends whose children are the same age as yours, you can set up your own play group. Start with four or five children, eighteen months or older, and plan to meet at least once a week, rotating from house to house. Be sure that the children like to play together, however, to avoid clashes later on.

Membership in a play group will give you several mornings of free time in return for one morning's strenuous activity. The supervising parent supplies a mid-morning snack, as well as toys, crayons, play dough, backyard sandbox, or wading pool. Parents drop off the children at an agreed time and return to pick them up a few hours later.

There are also drop-in centres all across Canada, which function as an informal babysitting service. Most centres have at least one trained staff member on hand to give professional advice, but they mainly function as a place to go, a comfortable, toy-filled refuge where preschoolers are welcome and parents can meet and socialize.

The Children's Storefront in Toronto began in 1976 as a toy lending centre. Then director Ryva Novick discovered that parents didn't really want to take toys home. They preferred to stay there, trading stories and experiences with other parents, while their children played. What they needed was a respite from the boredom and isolation of being home alone with a small child.

A babysitting co-operative is a more formal type of exchange. The group should not be too large—between 10 to 20 members is probably ideal. Members should be compatible with each other and have similar ideas about childrearing. For the sake of convenience, they should live within easy reach of one another.

Play Groups and Co-ops, cont'd:

In a babysitting co-op, no money changes hands — only tickets or cards that represent time. Free child care isn't the only benefit. You can meet other neighbourhood parents, with whom you can share clothes, toys, and parenting tips. And your child meets some playmates, who become increasingly important as the baby gets older.

To survive and flourish, a babysitting co-op needs clear and firm ground rules. Once you have a group of interested parents, you should have a meeting to decide on certain issues:

- How will you keep track of sitting time?
- Does the child go to the sitter's house or vice versa?
- What is the maximum age of children and the maximum number of children per family?
- How often will the group meet?
- How will new members be recruited?
- What happens if the babysitter has to cancel at the last minute?
- What is the penalty, if any, for members who don't pull their own weight?

Babysitting co-ops usually have a secretary who acts as an intermediary. The secretary calls other members to find a sitter when someone makes a request and keeps records of debits and credits. Members are issued a number of tickets (say 20 hours' worth) when they join and must return these tickets to the co-op when they leave.

carefully for hidden messages. People often say more than they realize.

What is their attitude towards babysitting? If a caller seems disappointed to hear that your baby doesn't sleep most of the day, it's a sign that this sitter won't enjoy caring for an active infant.

Using the information you obtain over the phone, you can prepare a short list of promising candidates. When you set up appointments with prospective babysitters, make sure each one is at a time when your baby is awake and alert. You want to see the interaction between the two of them.

Interviews with potential babysitters are usually in your home, unless the sitter is offering care in her own home. In that case, you want to assess the home and see if it meets your standards. Teenage babysitters should also be interviewed in their own homes, so you have an opportunity to meet their parents and discuss transportation and hours. Knowing a teen's parents can help if any problems arise later.

When you interview candidates, ask yourself some questions. Did the sitter arrive on time? Do you feel comfortable with her? Is she natural and at ease with your child? How does your child respond to her?

The best test is to excuse yourself for a few minutes during the interview and leave the sitter alone with the child. Make sure you can hear how they react, or fail to react, to each other, without being observed. If the sitter makes no effort to interact with the baby while you are gone, it doesn't bode well.

Always ask for references. (In the case of a teenager, references can come from a teacher or principal, as well as from other parents.) Once you get the names and phone numbers of former employers, try to call them. Here are some questions to ask:

- Would you hire this person again?
- What was her relationship with the children? Were they glad to see her come and sad to see her go?
- Did she always arrive on time?
- Was she easy to get along with?
- Did she seem to enjoy the work?

If the sitter can't supply references, ask her to come in for a try-out. She can look after the baby while you prepare dinner and monitor her performance, or you can zip out for some quick shopping and still be close enough to check up if you're nervous. Another good trial is an outing. Take the sitter along as an extra helper, maybe half-price for this one trial.

When interviewing a sitter, ask not only about previous experience but about child-rearing philosophy and attitudes. Why does she want to take care of children? How does she see her potential role?

Does she understand the need to stimulate your child's curiosity? And more important, does she know how to do it? (Rule out the candidate who immediately answers, "Don't you have a playpen?")

How would she handle temper tantrums, prolonged crying, failure to eat or sleep? What are her views about discipline?

Try to establish whether the person is rigid or flexible. Are your child-caring styles compatible?

Be sure to ask "what if" questions. What if the baby rolls off the changing table and bumps her head? What if there's a fire in the kitchen and it starts to fill up with smoke? You may feel foolish asking these questions, but it's often surprising what people don't know.

When you have interviewed a number of candidates, decide which one comes closest to your ideal caregiver. Did one person score high on all counts—experience, references, rapport with your child, similar views on child-rearing?

Which person did you like best? With whom did you feel most comfortable? These considerations are subjective, but they're significant. Rely on your instincts. Chances are, if you don't like the person, neither will your child.

BEFORE YOU LEAVE

All sitters, especially teenagers, need to know what they can and can't do at your house. Compile a list of rules ahead of time and give it to the sitter before you go out. To prepare the list, ask yourself questions like these:

- Do you allow smoking? Only in certain rooms? Only when

the baby is asleep? Should the ashtrays be washed out and the butts thrown away?

- Do you allow any drinking of liquor? Beer?
- Can the sitter make herself a snack? Which foods are allowed and which foods are off limits? Should she wash any dishes she has used?
- Can she invite friends over after the baby is asleep? How many? Can she go to sleep herself later, or do you expect her to stay awake and alert?
- Can she watch TV, listen to the stereo, read your magazines and books?
- Can she talk on the telephone? How long should her personal telephone calls last? If there are calls for you, what should she say? (Instead of saying you're not home, she might be instructed to say that you can't answer the phone right now and will call back later.) How should she handle messages?
- If the doorbell rings, should she open the door?
- If there are any pets, should they be fed, let in or out, leashed?

Besides rules for the babysitter, your child probably has routines which you want the sitter to observe. Explain them before you go and maybe write them down as well. For example:

- Can your child have a bottle while you are out? If you are breastfeeding, should the babysitter avoid giving a bottle until you arrive home?
- How should the sitter handle a crying spell? Does your child like special comforting? A rocking chair session, a favourite music box, a few minutes in the automatic swing?
- When, where, and how often should diapers be changed? Where do you keep the diapers? Rubber pants? Are there any ointments or creams? Where and how should diapers be thrown away?

- Do you want the sitter to give your child a bath? Wash her hair? Where is the child's towel, nightwear? Does she have baby powder after the bath?
- Do you want the sitter to give the child any medicine? If so, how? In a nipple, a special medicine spoon, an ordinary teaspoon or tablespoon, mixed with applesauce or jam? When and how often should medicine be given?

For older children, you should cover the following questions:

- How much television can the child watch? Which programs are allowed and which are not?
- When is the child's naptime? Bedtime? Does she sleep with a night light? Is the door open or shut? Any special routines?
- What time are the child's meals? Where are they eaten? Are there any special dishes or utensils? Any vitamins?
- Can the child have snacks between meals? Which foods are allowable and which are not? Clearly identify foods your child does not like or to which she is allergic.
- Can the child play outdoors? Can she go to other children's homes? Can other children come to your home? Which activities are allowed and which are not?
- Do you expect the child to tidy up her own toys at the end of the day? If not, should the sitter do it?

If your child is just learning to talk, make a list of the words she uses for favourite toys or foods. Without the translation of these special words, it can be a frustrating experience for the child and sitter alike. Your word list should have two columns: (1) If It Sounds Like, and (2) It Means. Then all the sitter has to do is check the list to find out that "nummies" means food, or "ba" means blanket. (Keep the list as a childhood memento.)

Tell the sitter about the baby's stage of development ("stands up but can't sit down") and current mischief, such as pulling books off shelves. Make sure you mention any special fears or routines ("don't turn out the hallway light," "wind up musical mobile before bedtime") and the location of all baby supplies. If the medicine chest has a childproof latch on it, show the sitter how it works.

As for payment, the best way to determine how much to pay a sitter is to ask your friends the going rate. Sometimes it's customary to pay more for daytime sitting as opposed to the easier nighttime variety. Negotiate a rate in advance that is acceptable to you both and, when dealing with younger teenagers, it's probably best to run through the arrangement with their parents so everything is clear.

Ask about a young sitter's curfew and if you're unavoidably delayed, call your sitter (and her parents too if possible). You should supply a modest bonus if you're late; likewise if the sitter did some housework, or if your child wasn't feeling well and was difficult to settle down. And if you have a steady arrangement with a sitter and have to cancel at the last minute, you should offer a few dollars for the inconvenience.

For a good sitter, it's probably wise to offer a raise after a few months. You can't skimp on quality help. Babysitters are in demand and there are dozens of other parents who are anxious to find one. If your own sitter feels well treated, she will stay loyal to you.

EMERGENCIES

Before you go out, take the sitter on a house tour, showing her the location of rooms, telephone, light switches, exits, door locks and extra keys, thermostats, fire extinguishers or smoke alarms, fuse boxes, and extra fuses. In case of a power blackout, keep a flashlight handy, or some candles and matches.

It's extremely important to let the babysitter know how your house works. Every home has its idiosyncrasies. If the house has an eccentric wiring system, for instance, with one fuse that is easy to blow, tell her. Otherwise you're likely to return home and find her waiting nervously in the dark for you.

If you expect the babysitter to use any household appliances, leave instructions on how to operate them (and what to do if they *don't* work).

For household emergencies, leave a list of phone numbers near the telephone. Note where you can be reached—or if you can't be, leave the number of a relative or a neighbour. Include phone numbers for the police, fire department, ambulance, and poison control.

As an extra precaution, write out your name, address, phone number, the child's weight, and complete and simple directions to your house. That way, anyone calling for help will be sure to relay this information quickly and correctly.

In case of fire, you should have an emergency routine worked out and be sure that your babysitter is familiar with your plan. Emphasize that this is no time for heroic measures— she should follow your instructions exactly.

For medical emergencies, leave the phone number of your doctor, dentist and the nearest hospital. Write out the child's full name, birth date, details of medical insurance coverage, and the location of first-aid supplies such as syrup of ipecac (to induce vomiting). The babysitter, however, should *not* give any medication unless specifically told to do so by a doctor or poison control centre.

Remind the sitter of any allergies or health-related conditions your child may have and show her where to look for first-aid information. Dr. Spock's *Baby and Child Care*, a book found in most households, is helpful and has a whole chapter on first aid. Another useful source is *Dear Baby-sitter*, a sitter's handbook and notebook compiled by Vicki Lansky.

Leave a consent form with your sitter, giving her permission to authorize emergency medical treatment for your child in your absence. Here's a sample:

"_____ has my permission to consent to emergency medical treatment where the need for such treatment is immediate and efforts to contact me are unsuccessful."

Signed _____ Date _____
Child's doctor _____
Child's relatives _____

In an emergency, your babysitter may need money for a taxi fare or drug prescription, so leave some spare change around the house and show the sitter where it is before you go out. She'll appreciate your thoughtfulness.

Preparing a new babysitter takes time, so you should avoid last-minute dashes. If you're going out at 8 p.m., ask the sitter to arrive at 7:00 or 7:30. This will allow you to familiarize the sitter with your child and your house — and to get dressed without having to attend to the baby at the same time.

SAYING GOODBYE

Before eight or nine months, your baby will not seem to notice when you leave. But as she grows, she not only begins to notice, she begins to care, sometimes very much indeed. Soon she will be crying and clinging to your leg, screaming as if she were seeing you for the last time and you were never coming back.

Fortunately, once you're out of the house, the baby often accepts, and even enjoys, a substitute caregiver. But she'll do this more readily if she's left with someone familiar and you do not disappear without warning. While it's tempting to do so, never sneak out of the house. Always say goodbye before you leave, assuring your child you will be back soon.

If you're worried, you can wait outside the door till the crying stops. It inevitably does within a few minutes, a half-hour at the most. Call later to see how things are going and if you have any doubts, return unannounced.

Never cancel your plans because your baby screams when you go. The parent who stays home out of guilt or concern when a toddler cries may be confirming the child's fears. To the child, it may seem that you are agreeing with her, saying "You're right, leaving *is* too scary for you to cope with so I'd better stay home." In contrast, the parent who calmly leaves, while sympathizing with the child, may be telling her, "I know it's hard, but I have confidence in your ability to get along without me for a little while."

Though saying goodbye is never easy, there are ways to make a leave-taking less painful:

• Before you leave your child with a new babysitter, invite the sitter to your house for a meal or a visit. The child will feel more comfortable getting to know the sitter while you are still there.

• If you can't arrange a prior visit, make sure the sitter arrives before your child goes to bed. She may get frightened if she wakes up to find a stranger hovering over her crib.

• If you're leaving your child at the sitter's house, visit her beforehand with your child. Familiarity helps. When you leave your child there, remember to bring a talisman from home — a blanket or favourite toy or book.

• Plan something special for the child to do with the sitter. Before you go, help them get started on an enjoyable activity such as water play, painting, or cooking.

• Arrange to have the sitter give something special to your child. A new toy or favourite snack usually works well. Some sitters come equipped with a grab-bag of toys and treasures to pacify and distract a child who is feeling abandoned.

• A good prevention technique is to forewarn. At least fifteen minutes before you go, tell your child you will be leaving soon. Let her get used to the idea, so it won't come as a complete surprise.

• Develop a leave-taking ritual. Suggest that she wave goodbye at the window with her sitter after you say goodbye at the door, for instance. This second goodbye will give her something to do immediately and help her feel more in control of the situation. Other traditions you could start: a special kiss, a secret farewell gesture, a parting knock on the door when you are outside. You could also try a homecoming ritual too, that corresponds with the one you use when you leave.

Once your child learns to talk, never lie to her about the fact that you're going out or how long you'll be gone. Your child is learning to trust you, and it's important not to destroy this growing trust, even if you have to start an evening of fun by leaving behind a screaming child.

Always tell your child you will return. Saying, "I will come back later" as you leave and "I came back" when you return teaches your toddler that you will not abandon her.

Since young children have a hazy idea of time, speak to them in terms of activities. Instead of saying you'll be back in two hours, say you'll be back after snack time or after naptime.

Finally, remain calm, reassuring, and stable yourself, whatever happens. Express sympathy for your child's feelings, but don't allow her tears to change your mind about leaving.

These leave-taking strategies will come in handy when you decide to go back to work. Since formal day care for infants is very limited, you may hire a babysitter instead. Leaving your baby then will be easier if she already knows the routine.

CHAPTER 12

Child Care

WHO WILL LOOK after the baby?

That's the first question you will be asked when you announce that you are going back to work. Your answer will probably reflect long, hard thought and some tough decisions.

Of all the choices a new parent must make, this one is the most vital. Your infant isn't likely to notice that the wallpaper you chose for the nursery isn't washable after all. Nor will he care that the $300 made-in-England pram you bought turned out to be a dud. But the arrangements you make for child care will matter to your baby every day.

Combining work and childrearing is a fact of life for most Canadian mothers. Right now the prospect of juggling job and baby may not appeal to you. The frantic first weeks you had at home with your infant are finally being replaced by a calmer pace and perhaps you and the baby are just getting to know one another. You might be enjoying a more leisurely lifestyle and the pressure of work suddenly has no appeal.

Doubts about leaving your child to someone else's care may also make you hesitate. What if the baby doesn't get enough attention? How can anyone else be as loving towards our baby as we are? What if we choose the wrong kind of care?

One new mother in her mid-30s was surprised by her own

reluctance to return to work. "From the time I learned I was pregnant I had planned to rush right back to work when the baby was three months old. I assumed I'd be terribly bored. But when the time came I found myself wishing I could stay at home longer. Jon was just settling down and I was really enjoying him."

Mixed feelings about returning to work are to be expected. But you will find the transition much easier if you are happy with the child care arrangements you make. Early planning is essential, because there are many options to choose from and you'll want to avoid a last-minute compromise.

Once you make your decision and are back at work, be prepared for a period of adjustment as you, your partner, and the baby get used to the new arrangements. Establishing a different routine takes a few weeks, particularly if you are relying on care outside your home. The time involved in transporting the baby back and forth can shorten the day significantly and household chores, which multiply when a baby is added to the family unit, must be jammed into the precious evening hours or weekends.

In these early weeks, take plenty of shortcuts. Follow the same survival plan you used when you arrived home from the hospital. Keep cooking to a minimum, for instance, even if it means making take-out food part of your daily menu. Don't schedule any evening activities until you are really ready for them. Let the laundry pile up. (Invest in extra clothing for the baby instead.) Temporary chaos is inevitable. Concentrate instead on spending time with your child and unwinding from the workday. As the weeks pass you will become more organized and day-to-day life will grow more manageable.

The day care debate is loud and passionate. Critics of working parents claim that being separated from the parents jeopardizes the infant's intellectual and emotional development. A child left in another's care, some experts assert, has serious problems forming attachments to his own parents.

The nurturing an infant needs must be provided by the parent, not a substitute.

Lined up on the other side of the fence are the child care experts and educators who maintain that it is the quality of the time spent with the child, not the quantity, which matters. Children are adaptable, they respond to loving care from anyone, not just their parents, and a mother and father happy in their work and cheerfully affectionate at home offer a healthy environment to their child.

Arguments like these may seem academic to most of us, who work out of economic necessity, and are not allowed the luxury of a choice. In fact, the debate in Canada now focuses on the right to affordable, high-quality day care. The issue is no longer whether child care programs are needed, but instead how they should be funded, expanded, and improved. See page 178–179 for more on Canadian child care changes.

But concern about your absence and its effect on your baby remains, no matter why you work or who cares for your child.

There is a substantial body of research on the impact of day care which indicates that children of working parents show no ill effects from the experience when their care has been of high quality. In fact, many studies clearly demonstrate that infants cared for in a good day care centre and those reared at home follow similar paths in their social, personal, and intellectual growth. Often a woman can be a better mother because she also has a career outside the home.

Another critical point to remember when you are making decisions about child care is the importance of consistent care. Your child will feel more secure — no matter how young he is — when he is cared for by the same person. Unfortunately, disruptions sometimes can't be helped. Nannies quit, you decide you aren't satisfied with the neighbourhood centre, you move to a new city or neighbourhood, etc. But a change in child care should not be made lightly. A stable child care arrangement is essential.

LICENSED OR UNLICENSED CARE

Right at the beginning of your search, you will have to decide between licensed and unlicensed care. There are two forms of licensed care. The most common is the licensed child care centre. Less well known is child care provided in a licensed home.

All provinces and territories (except for the Northwest Territories, which has no child care legislation) license day care centres. Provincial laws regulate not only physical requirements for day care centres, but also staff/child ratios and educational requirements for child care workers. The main advantages of licensed centre care over other options are safety, staff qualifications, and reliability.

Licensed family home day care, while representing a very small share of the licensed market, is available in all provinces and territories except New Brunswick, Newfoundland and the Northwest Territories. Licensing requirements for family homes vary from province to province, but are generally much less stringent than those for day care centres.

One major difference between the two is in the area of training. Although several provinces have started to provide training for family home day care providers, none requires licensed family home workers to have any formal training in child care or child development.

The advantage of licensed family homes is that they may offer more flexible hours than day care centres do. And they provide care in a home setting, which some parents prefer.

Whether in a day care centre or family home, licensed care is usually more attractive than unlicensed care. A 1986 task force on child care headed by Katie Cooke found in its surveys that the majority of Canadian parents prefer licensed child care for children of all ages. Licensed care

Licensed or Unlicensed Care, cont'd.:

is subject to minimum standards, while unlicensed care varies in quality from good to extremely poor.

"There is no system of quality control upon which parents can rely," the task force report said about unlicensed care. "Parents must trust their own judgment about the appropriateness and quality of unlicensed care, and they have little opportunity to monitor the quality of care their child is receiving during the day."

Although licensed care is preferable, it is shockingly scarce in Canada, especially for infants. A study by the National Day Care Information Centre in 1986 showed that less than 7 percent of children under eighteen months, and less than 14 percent of those from eighteen to thirty-five months, whose parents worked or studied a substantial part of the week could be cared for in licensed day care centres or licensed family homes.

One reason for the high demand is the shortage of infant centres. It is more difficult to place a child under three years of age in a group care setting. Most centres restrict their enrolment to children three to five, since infants require specialized care and a much higher adult/child ratio. Also, a few Canadian provinces do not allow group infant care. Newfoundland does not allow children under two in centres, and Saskatchewan and British Columbia do not allow children under eighteen months.

Licensed family home care is so rare in Canada that few parents seem to be aware of its existence. Letters from parents to the task force rarely mentioned this type of care, and most parents interviewed about their child care preferences were not familiar with it.

When you look for child care, use a consumer's perspective. Centres can be housed in a church basement, a high-rise, an elementary school, high school or university, or a community centre. They can be commercially run, with names like Kiddie Kare, or run by the government. Non-profit centres are often operated by churches and community groups.

Find out exactly what services are available to you, which one is most appropriate and which offers the best value — for all of you. Consider your needs, your infant's and your partner's. (It has been pointed out before that it is not unusual for parents to spend more time choosing a new appliance than they do looking for good day care.)

If your working hours are unpredictable, for example, an individual caregiver may be preferable; the hours in which day care centres are open may not fit into your schedule. This can also hold true when you are working part-time, since centres frequently insist on full-time attendance.

Some parents find a child care "package" works well for them: a combination of arrangements. They may rely on a nursery for a few days a week, for instance, and on the remaining weekdays they leave their children with a sitter.

The options in child care arrangements can be overwhelming at first. Take the time to investigate them thoroughly and choose with caution. You are making one of your most important investments ever.

Believe it or not, the ideal time to begin looking at day care centres is while you're pregnant, if not before. The best centres have long waiting lists and it is not unusual for a child to join the list months before he has even emerged from the womb.

CHILD CARE CENTRES

Child care centres offer group care for infants and pre-schoolers. Most provide a structured program with outdoor and indoor play, storytime, arts and crafts, and nutritious meals and snacks. They are usually open from 7:30 a.m. to 5:30 or 6 p.m.

Although day care centres are licensed, the quality of care

varies considerably. Even licensed care does not always mean good care. A number of centres don't meet minimum provincial standards and parents don't complain, either because they don't know what the law requires, or because they are frightened of losing their children's places and ending up without child care.

Provincial inspectors are supposed to visit day care centres regularly to make sure they are operating within the law. However, enforcement is often lax because of the scarcity of day care. The inspectors are faced with the choice of either closing down the centre or closing their eyes to some violations.

Licensing is not a guarantee of top-quality care, but it is at least a start. If you intend to enrol your child in day care, get a copy of the provincial regulations on the centre's physical surroundings, health, safety, nutrition, emergency procedures, staff/child ratios, staff training, and other related concerns. (Call your provincial government switchboard for information.)

Remember that standards are minimum only. Some centres will only meet the standards, others surpass these minimums in one or more areas. When shopping for a child care arrangement, keep in mind not only licensing requirements but also specific features that matter to you — such variables as staff qualifications, group size, staff/child ratios, the type of programming, and the willingness of centres to involve parents.

The sponsorship of day care centres is a controversial issue. Non-profit centres are generally sponsored either by community organizations such as churches or charities, or parent co-operatives, run by parents of children in the centre. In two provinces, Alberta and Ontario, a number of municipalities operate day care centres for children in their communities. And there are commercial centres, run by individual businesses, chains, or franchise operations. One thing you should be aware of is the lower pay scale in commercial centres. The federal task force on child care found that staff in centres operated for a profit earned 30 percent less than staff in non-profit centres, and 50 percent less than staff who worked in municipal centres. (New federal funding for child care centres, however, is expected to improve staff salaries.)

In 1986, publicly-operated child care centres accounted for less than 14 percent of spaces in Canada. Most centres are privately run either by non-profit groups and organizations (48 percent) or by private businesses (38 percent).

Parent-run centres are also usually non-profit. They can be either run and staffed by parents, or run by the parents but staffed by professionals hired by the parents. Most such co-operatives rely on parents to contribute their time to the centre — a certain number of hours per day or month — which allows them to cut down on expenses and charge lower fees.

Parent co-ops are run by groups who share the same general philosophies about child care. If you are considering joining such a centre, get to know the other parents. Attend a few meetings and see how the centre functions during the day. Be sure you agree with the group's childrearing attitudes. Find out exactly what is required from each parent in terms of time and tasks.

When co-ops are well run and the parent group is compatible, they can be the answer to a parent's prayer. The level of commitment, the sense of shared values, the friendly, communal spirit make such centres a special breed.

Andy, a single parent, is delighted with the co-op he has found. "I like the fact that I have a say in every decision that's made, from the food we buy for the kids to the educational philosophy. In the centre my daughter was in before, I picked her up and dropped her off and barely knew who took care of her. Here we're like a family."

"Our co-op got started because we had lots of working parents in the neighbourhood but not enough day care," says Sue, a teacher and mother of two pre-schoolers. "We got together and persuaded a local school to donate their unused classrooms to us. We worked nights and weekends to fix up the rooms so the space was practical for younger children. But after the centre opened, the group started having problems. Not all of us agreed on how to run the program. Some wanted more structure, others wanted less. Deciding how to restrict enrolment was a real debate. Meetings turned into arguments. My husband and I ended up leaving and looking for a less political day care situation."

How do you find a good infant centre? Ask friends, relatives, and neighbours for recommendations. Talk to your colleagues. Phone City Hall. Visit the neighbourhood community centre, the local Y, the library, and the women's centre in your area. Read the bulletin boards at the supermarket and laundromat. Check the newspaper classifieds, and the yellow pages under "Day Nurseries." Your community may also have a day care action group that can offer you advice.

Once you have a list of centres, start making phone calls. You will be able to save yourself a lot of time in wasted visits by using the telephone to screen the prospective centres. But before you even start dialling, make sure that your list is limited to centres that are conveniently located.

Ask the staff member at each centre about the centre's hours of operation. How much does it cost? How is it funded? Is it licensed? Are there any openings now, and if not when is there likely to be one? Mention the age of your child — or what age your infant will be when you are ready to enrol him. Find out what ages of children the centre cares for. Point out any special health problems your child has.

Encourage the worker or administrator to talk about the centre and its program. And make a note of the information you are given and your impression of the person's attitude. While it's not fair to rule out a centre if you happen to encounter an impatient or unhelpful staff member, you may want to make sure that this attitude isn't typical of the centre's staff. (It's worth remembering, however, that the centre's priority should be its children and if conversation is cut short

NEW CHILD CARE POLICY

For the first time, the federal government has turned its attention to the need for action on child care. The federal Conservative government, after a decade of study and five years of loud public debate, presented a $6.4-billion national strategy in late 1987. But the plan was hotly criticized by provincial officials and child care advocates alike.

While it is intended to double the number of day care spaces from 200,000 to 400,000 by 1995, the proposed Canada Child Care Act does not establish minimum national standards for day care centres. It also imposes a new ceiling on provincial spending for subsidized day care spaces, replacing the former open-ended cost-sharing scheme between Ottawa and the provinces, and acting as a straitjacket for provinces' plans to expand their programs.

As well, the Act allows commercial centres to qualify for federal funding, despite the fact that studies have shown commercial care to be inferior to that provided in non-profit centres. These new federal dollars may open the door for U.S. profit-making "McDaycare" chains, particularly with the arrival of free trade.

New tax breaks for parents — an increase in both deductions and credits — were also introduced as part of Ottawa's tax reform measures. Tax benefits will double federal tax deductions to $4,000 for each child under age seven in a family, without the former ceiling of $8,000. This applies, however, only to those parents who have receipts for their children's care.

Families with young children at home can receive increased tax credits, which decline in value as earnings rise. A family earning up to $24,000, for example, could receive a rebate of $624 per child in 1988, $724 in 1989.

The tax credit is designed to recognize the expenses of parents who stay at home to raise their children, or who cannot obtain a receipt from their caregivers. Many work-

New Child Care Policy, cont'd:

ing parents fall into this latter category because they depend on unlicensed care. But the new system of credits allows them only minor tax relief. Thus the system favours families with higher incomes, who can afford the type of care that furnishes them with receipts (child care centres or nannies) — in other words, the families who need a tax break the least.

Although the Conservatives were anxious to pass the child care bill before the federal election in late 1988, the Senate did not approve it in time. The bill died with the election call in October. The Liberal and New Democrat parties were quick to condemn the scheme and proposed their own solutions, should they win the election. The New Democrats promised to spend less money and produce the same number of spaces as the Conservative policy, with a shorter timetable; the Liberals said they would spend more than the other two parties and create double the number of new spaces.

But the issue of free trade managed to eclipse the child care controversy during the provocative federal election campaign. The Conservatives were returned to power with a strong majority. At the time that this book went to press, the controversial child care bill, despite its flaws, was expected to be reintroduced and passed as quickly as possible. And unless the Canada Child Care Act is greatly improved before it passes, Canadian working parents will find themselves not much closer to the goal of accessible, affordable, quality child care.

because it interferes with child care, that's a point in the centre's favour.)

If you are satisfied with the information you gather, set up an appointment to visit the centre. Avoid an interview time at the start or end of the day, since the staff will be preoccupied with the children's arrivals and departures and you won't be able to see what the centre's program is like.

Allow at least an hour for your visit, and preferably two, to observe the centre properly. If you can, hold the interview in an area where the infants are cared for, rather than a private office. This means that you can take stock of the centre while you chat.

With day care centres, observing matters more than interviewing. But your questions should count.

Ask about the centre's philosophy. Does the answer cover only health and safety, or are stimulation, emotional security, and affection also discussed? Are you hearing a lot of jargon? If so, be suspicious. You aren't looking for textbook answers.

How long has the centre been open? What is the adult/child ratio? Because infants demand more individualized care, the ratio should be higher than in day care centres for older children. One adult to three or four infants is an acceptable ratio. Ask about group size.

Ask the director of the centre to describe a typical day. Inquire about staff turnover, and how staff is chosen. Are there parent meetings? What is the staff's training?

Discuss the fees, when they are due, and how they are paid. What financial arrangements are made if your child cannot attend for a while? Make sure you know the centre's hours of operation. Is there any flexibility?

Ask to meet one or two of the staff, so you can hear their views about their work. Talk about your baby, his schedule, his likes, and dislikes. How does the staff respond?

Your visit should include a tour of the centre, and make your tour effective. Keep these points in mind.

- What kind of equipment does the centre have? How well is it maintained? Is it safe? Is there enough?
- Is the centre bright and attractive and well cared for? Does it seem comfortable? Are there windows? Do you notice any smells?

FINDING GOOD DAY CARE

Research on day care centres has isolated six key elements of high-quality care:

1. Staff/child ratios.

   Lower ratios usually mean a lower standard of care because of the decreasing ability of the staff to provide each child with the necessary amount of individual attention. The recommended ratio for children under three years of age is one adult for every three children.

2. Group size.

   The group must be small enough to allow caregivers to manage both individual and group activities. For children under three, the optimal group size is six children with two staff members.

3. Caregiver qualifications.

   Studies have shown that neither formal education nor the length of work experience in child care contribute significantly to the quality of caregiver/child interactions. What really matters is the training related to early childhood development and child care. Motivation, communication skills, and enjoyment of children are also important.

4. Curriculum.

   There are several approaches to early childhood education. In a highly structured program, children tend to show less independence and initiative, but do better on achievement and intelligence tests. In a less structured program, children are often more independent and persistent and tend to do well on tests of inventiveness and problem-solving. Some experts feel that the effort to define a program may be more important to its quality than the program's specific content.

5. Physical environment.

   The overall size of a centre, space, design and layout

Finding Good Day Care, cont'd:

of space, and availability of materials also influence children's experiences in child care. Indoor space should be well-ventilated, include some natural light, meet requirements for health, safety, and fire standards, and lend itself to both group and individual play. Materials should be available in sufficient quantities to allow choices by the children and avoid unnecessary competition.

6. Parent involvement.

Research shows that children's developmental gains are strengthened when programs involve parents, and when there is continuity between home and centre environments. Parents can provide direct support to staff by participating on an advisory board, acting as volunteers within the program, or contributing money and equipment.

The stability of the arrangement is also significant. Frequent changes in child care arrangements are very upsetting for both children and parents. In day care centres, poor quality care is often associated with a high staff turnover rate. For infants and toddlers, look for centres with low staff turnover.

- Does each child have his own crib?
- Does the staff appear happy? How do they relate to the babies in their care? Are they affectionate or just efficient? Do they seem rushed? Relaxed? Bored? How much do they touch the infants? Play with them?
- Are babies held when they are fed?
- What is the response to a crying infant?
- Are the babies fed and changed promptly?
- Do the toddlers at the centre receive enough attention?
- Do gates protect stairways and unsupervised areas?

- What kinds of toys do you notice? Are there mobiles, pictures, music boxes? What do the infants in the centre's cribs see?
- Is there enough space? Does the centre appear cramped?

Follow your intuition when you evaluate each centre. You don't have to be a child care professional to distinguish a good centre from a bad one. Trust your instincts. What was your overall impression of the centre? Imagine leaving your child here every morning—what's your gut reaction?

It may take a few visits before you happen on an acceptable centre, so don't be discouraged if you don't like the first centre you visit. It *is* possible to find a high-quality child care centre, as plenty of parents will attest. Discovering a warm, enthusiastic, caring staff who run a top-notch program makes the search worth every minute.

"Our son has been at a day care centre in our neighbourhood since he was three-and-a-half months old," says Linda. "I went from one centre to another and wasn't getting anywhere. One was dirty and dingy, another was overcrowded. But finally I heard about this one from someone at work. The staff is just excellent and we couldn't be happier. Lots of people—including my mother—have let us know that they don't approve of day care for babies of Jeremy's age. But he's getting loads of attention and I feel better knowing that I can rely on the centre. They're not going to call me one morning and say that they're sick and can't look after him today!"

If the day care centre you prefer has no openings, ask to be added to its waiting list. Make interim arrangements for your baby's care. Then don't let the staff forget about you. Call them regularly to see if any openings have materialized.

Don't forget, too, that even though many centres don't accept children under two years of age, you may want to enrol your child when he reaches the appropriate age. So it's worthwhile to keep in touch with the available centres, keep abreast of any new ones, and ask to be added to a waiting list if necessary.

FAMILY DAY CARE

This is the most common form of child care. Parents use friends, relatives, or neighbours, or they find someone through newspaper ads or bulletin boards.

Many working parents prefer a family setting near their home. The hours offer a flexibility day care centres lack. And family day care is low-cost, less expensive than a centre and less than half the price of in-home care. It's also easier to find this kind of care than it is to locate day care centres, which are in short supply.

Word of mouth is a common way parents find a neighbourhood caregiver. Let your friends and neighbours know you're looking; ask other parents to make suggestions. Place a newspaper ad or post a notice at the local community centre, women's centre, library, or supermarket. Find out if your community has a day care action group. Some communities print babysitters' directories. You can also contact local schools and churches.

Screen the phone calls you receive. Outline the hours you need care for your child. Ask about experience. How many other children are in her care? (Provincial laws restrict the number of children per home for this type of care.) The maximum number of children allowed in a family day care home in most provinces is in the range of three to five preschoolers.

You should make at least two visits to the caregiver's home. Information on interviewing appears later in this chapter. Aside from personally evaluating the caregiver, however, you will need to inspect her home and be confident that the setting is satisfactory for your child.

The best arrangement is licensed family day care, but these homes are in the minority. They *can* be found, however — more easily in cities than in smaller communities. Contact a community information centre or your local social services department.

Also desirable is a family day care home sponsored by an agency or community group. Agency-sponsored family child care is found in Alberta, Ontario, Quebec, and Nova Scotia. When a home is supervised, it must meet health and safety standards and the caregiver is screened, approved, and visited regularly. She is often offered training and advice on child care. Some agencies run caregiver drop-ins; toy and book-lending libraries are another resource, and advice is available to the caregiver in case of emergency. Studies have shown that these caregivers see themselves as professionals. They pay more attention to child care, less to housework.

Though your judgment on a caregiver's quality is important in any setting, it becomes especially crucial in informal (i.e., unsupervised) family care. Good family day care can be a home away from home for your child. Bad family day care can be disastrous.

What you want to avoid is custodial care — a person who tends your baby between TV, phone calls, and naps. Your baby is too young to complain, so you have to trust your instincts and choose cautiously.

If possible, make your visit to the day-care person's home without your child. You will be free to talk and observe without distractions. Schedule your visit for a time when you can see the caregiver in action but not when she is too busy to talk to you.

Look around the home carefully while you interview her. Is the home clean? Clutter is normal — in fact it's a healthy sign in a child-centred home — but the bathrooms and kitchen should be sanitary.

How safe is the house? Is it childproofed? Are electrical outlets covered? Are dangerous objects out of reach?

Is there enough space for the number of children? Do they have a play area? Is there enough ventilation? What about toys and play equipment?

What is the home's atmosphere? Are there other adults?

Is there a fenced yard for the children? Does it have recreational facilities—swings, a sandbox, etc.? Are they safe?

What about the children now in her care? What is their attitude towards her—and hers towards them? Are they affectionate, nervous, lively, comfortable? How does she discipline them?

A second visit will let you see how the caregiver responds to your child. You can also exchange more detailed information about working hours, emergency arrangements, your child's schedule, his medical history, and the fees you will pay.

DOES THE DAY CARE HOME HAVE:

Enough furniture, playthings and other equipment for all the children in care?

Equipment that is safe and in good repair?

Enough room and cots or cribs so the children can take naps?

Safety caps on electrical outlets?

A safe place to store medicines, household cleansers, poisons, matches, sharp instruments, and other dangerous items?

An alternate exit in case of fire?

A safety plan to follow in emergencies?

An outdoor play area that is safe, fenced, and free of litter?

Enough heat, light, and ventilation?

Nutritious meals and snacks made from the kind of food you want your child to eat?

A first-aid kit? Fire extinguishers? Smoke detectors? Covered radiators and protected heaters? Covered screens or bars on windows above the first floor? Gates at tops and bottoms of stairs?

A clean and safe place to change diapers?

Before you hire her, check the caregiver's references thoroughly. Then confirm your arrangements in writing, summarizing the points you have agreed on.

Keep a good working relationship with your caregiver once you start leaving your child in her care. The women who do this work often complain of parents who are too rushed to sit down and talk. Make it a habit to let the caregiver know that you're pleased with her work. Allow a few minutes to chat about your child's day. Encourage her to share her observations with you. Report any change in your child's behaviour. And keep to the terms of your agreement, picking up and delivering your child punctually.

THE INTERVIEW

These are questions you'll need to ask a potential family caregiver. Many of them also apply to in-home care and to group care.

- What is your experience?
- What do you enjoy most about your job?
- How many children do you care for? What are their ages?
- How did you get started in this type of work?
- Describe a typical day's activities.
- How do you punish a child who misbehaves?
- How long do you plan to care for children?
- Have you had any special training?
- Do you have references?
- What happens if my child is ill?
- What happens if you are ill? Do you have a replacement lined up?
- Are any areas of your house out of bounds for the children?
- Where do they nap?
- Do you take vacations? When?

The Interview, cont'd:

- Have you ever had an emergency with a child? What happened? How did you handle it?
- What fire precautions have you taken?
- Where are emergency phone numbers kept?
- What would you do if my baby had a crying spell?
- What do you do to help a child adjust to your home at first?
- How do you feel about pacifiers? Demand feeding? Toilet training?
- Do you ever have to be away from the home? What arrangements do you make for the children's care?
- What are your fees? How do you like to be paid?
- Do you give receipts, so I can claim this expense on my income tax return?
- What if I'm late picking up the baby? Do you charge overtime?

Many parents find it helpful to pose "What if" questions: What if my baby fell off the changing table? What if he had a spell of colic? What if one of the children you look after became jealous of the attention you give my child?

Questions like these can help you to evaluate the caregiver's attitudes about childrearing. They can also give both of you the opportunity to establish a rapport and to see how compatible your views are.

If possible, leave your child alone for a few minutes with the person you're interviewing. Does the caregiver make contact with the baby?

Once you have found someone suitable, write a letter outlining your agreement. When you are hiring a live-in or live-out nanny, the agreement should be detailed, spelling out all the terms of her employment: hours, duties, salary, sick days, holidays. Define her duties as specifically as possible. For an example, see page 198.

WORKPLACE DAY CARE

For a handful of lucky working parents, their children are as near as the office elevator. These parents have the option of workplace day care — either on-site or nearby. A parent can spend the lunch hour visiting the child and a breastfeeding mother is able to nurse her infant.

Workplace day care is a new movement. It has benefits for both the employer (less absenteeism, reduced turnover, increased productivity, improved morale) and the employees (more time with their children, easier scheduling and commuting, reduced stress and less anxiety about child care). Fees are about the same as those in community-based day care centres. Employer contributions are usually in the form of capital, start-up, or occupancy costs, a relatively minor portion of the overall budget.

Most employer-supported programs in Canada are group child care centres at or near the workplace. However, employers may also purchase space at local centres or give direct subsidies to employees to help defray the cost of child care. Currently, there are about ninety employer-supported child care centres in Canada, mostly in Ontario and Quebec. Many of the programs provide infant care.

Child care counselling and referral services are a perk a few companies are starting to offer. The option is not as expensive for them as on-site day care, yet it answers a need employers are slowly recognizing. The services provide parents with individual consultations, free of charge, on their child care needs. It also refers them to the appropriate community services.

Check with your company's Human Resources Department about any programs available for working parents. If none exist, encourage the department to start one. Working parents are plentiful enough in any company to justify the expense and it is to your company's benefit to humanize the workplace and recognize the reality of child care concerns among their employees.

If your company does have an employer-sponsored day care centre, evaluate it with the same objectivity you would apply to any centre. (See pages 181-182.)

THE NANNY OR BABYSITTER

Nannies are expensive solutions to the child care dilemma, but their popularity is easy to understand. In a two-paycheque household, working hours are often long and unpredictable. Add a baby to the equation and the result can be chaos. Enter the live-in nanny, who restores organization, sanity, and convenience to the frantic working parents.

The traditional nanny is hard to find in Canada. Technically, "qualified" professional nannies have earned a certificate from the National Nursery Examination Board in Britain. The term "nanny" is now generic, however, usually referring to both live-in and live-out child care workers with training and/or experience. They can also be known as au pairs or mother's helpers.

In-home care has obvious advantages: no morning struggles to dress your child, feed him, deliver him to the centre or babysitter; no beat-the-clock return journeys at night to pick him up, rush home, stash his gear, and start dinner. You also have the reassurance of knowing that your infant is safe at home, in a warm, familiar setting, and, equally comforting, that he is being lovingly cared for in a one-to-one relationship.

It sounds wonderful. And for many working parents, it is. They have found the perfect nanny, their children are in capable hands and the household is running smoothly.

How did they find their treasures? Usually, not without a few mishaps along the way. Joy, a businesswoman and mother of eight-month-old Mark, describes her search.

"I hired a young girl who just did not work out. Basically she came to Canada to have a good time. We had a few horrific experiences with her and it became obvious that she wasn't looking after the baby properly.

"The agency suggested different methods of handling the problems between us but although their advice was good, I decided to let her go. I was only without a sitter for two days, luckily. Then they sent me Kathy, who I am delighted with." Other parents find that more than one nanny proves to be unsatisfactory before they finally discover a gem.

Before you start looking for a nanny—or housekeeper, or au pair or babysitter—decide what kind of household help you want. Is a live-in arrangement better for your needs or will you resent the lack of privacy? Is your home large enough to accommodate an extra person comfortably, or will your quarters be too cramped, with a daily line-up for the bathroom?

Many parents opt for live-out help but this means that they aren't able to count on evening or weekend babysitting. They also run the risk of coping with more "sick" days when the nanny can't make it to work. On the plus side, they maintain their privacy and are free of the demands of room and board.

You should also know the role you want your nanny to play. Do you want her to concentrate only on the baby or will you expect her to do light housekeeping, maybe even prepare dinner?

Money is an important issue too. Along with salary, there are the extra costs of room and board, medical insurance plans, unemployment insurance, workers' compensation, and Canada Pension payments.

By law, live-in nannies in Canada must be paid a minimum monthly wage which varies provincially. In Ontario, the rate is currently about $650 per month plus room and board. Many are paid more than this minimum amount — $1,000 monthly is not unusual — and wages are on the increase for qualified nannies as demand continues to climb.

You are expected to make deductions from your nanny's salary for income tax, unemployment insurance and Canada Pension Plan premiums. As her employer, you must pay a portion of her UIC and CPP premiums and you may also have to obtain Workers' Compensation coverage. As well, you will have to issue T4 forms and submit receipts to Revenue Canada. (Contact Revenue Canada to find out how to make these deductions from your nanny's salary.) A $4,000 portion of these child care costs is tax-deductible for each child. You are expected to keep records of the babysitter's name and address, date of employment, and wages for five years.

Budget ahead of time, so you know how much you can afford. As you can see, a nanny can cost a minimum of $8,000 a year plus room and board, and a live-out one can cost even more. Most live-out babysitters earn at least $200 a week. For middle-income earners, this is a sizable chunk out of their own salaries.

Some parents opt to share a nanny with working friends or neighbours who also have a child or two. The children enjoy daily playmates and the adults split the cost of the nanny's salary.

Language may be a factor in your requirements. When a caregiver doesn't speak English, you will find communication difficult (unless, of course, you can speak to her in her own language). This may mean that you won't be able to instruct her about your child's care in enough detail.

Do you want a young nanny, or an older woman? There are pros and cons for each. Younger nannies tend to change jobs regularly and often want an active social life. But they can also be energetic and refreshingly enthusiastic on the job. Mature women offer stability and if they live in they may be more willing to babysit on evenings and weekends.

Training is another issue. The traditional nanny is trained in child care. She views her work as a profession. Untrained caregivers can be equally competent but they are less likely to be committed to the job and may move on to greener pastures.

One mother is not impressed with formal training, however. "My husband and I decided that we didn't care if someone had a million qualifications. We wanted a certain personality. When we interviewed Shelley and asked her about experience, she pulled out a bunch of snapshots of the brothers and sisters she'd helped to raise in Mexico. That seemed like plenty of the right kind of experience. She's been with us nine months now, she's calm and easygoing and we are delighted with her."

You have done all the groundwork and you have a good idea of what you need. Now you are ready to start looking in earnest. Allow yourself enough time to find the right nanny, ideally at least two months (longer if you're sponsoring an overseas nanny). What you want to avoid is a hasty decision. Making a child care choice out of desperation is almost always a mistake.

Friends, neighbours, and relatives are your best resource, particularly if they have nannies themselves and are hooked into the nanny network. Spread the word that you are searching for a nanny.

Placement agencies find permanent or temporary household help for families. Some specialize in nannies, others place housekeepers, cleaning help, etc.

Check the yellow pages, under Domestic Help, Babysitters or Employment Agencies. Other working parents may be able to make suggestions about reliable agencies.

A few nanny agencies even specialize in particular nationalities. British nannies are popular and Canadian parents also show a preference for nannies from the Philippines. Canadian-trained nannies are in great demand, but unfortunately there aren't enough to go around. Foreign nannies are the norm.

If you decide to hire a certain nanny from abroad, you will have to wait at least three months while the immigration department approves your choice and issues the appropriate work permit to her. (Nannies who come on work permits can apply for permanent residency after they have been here for two years. During that period they are required to live with their employers.) But sometimes an agency will already have nannies here in Canada who are unhappy with their current families and want to change jobs. These nannies can be hired immediately though they will have to give their current employers enough time to replace them. Some agencies offer a share-a-nanny service, pairing parents in the same area with one nanny. Outline your requirements to each agency you contact. Good agencies will ask you for lots of details about your needs, so they can match the right nanny to the right family.

Why use an agency? Agencies can save you time. They screen their applicants and when nannies are imported, they handle some of the red tape. You can check out how thorough their screening techniques are by asking to see the files for a few of their nannies.

Critics of agencies maintain that agencies are more concerned with their commissions than with careful, sensitive matching of nanny and client. They sometimes ignore a nanny's preferences (number of children, non-smoking household) or overlook a client's special needs in their zeal to fill a vacancy. However, many parents are fully satisfied with the agencies they used.

"I'm glad I went to an agency," says Joy. "The one I used took time to find out what I wanted and gave me three or four references. She spent a long time with me even before I decided to choose her agency. Other people I know haven't been as pleased with their agencies but this one was excellent.

"My sister tried the classified ads and she has been through four or five nannies already. One left suddenly, one became pregnant, and so on. When my first nanny didn't work out, the agency replaced her quickly and reduced their fee."

Agencies charge a finder's fee. It can vary from 10 percent of the nanny's wage for four months, if it's a temporary placement, up to a month's salary for a permanent nanny. Ask about additional charges for expenses like telegrams, long-distance calls, and postage.

Agencies usually guarantee their placement for a specific period. Compare their guarantees. If the nanny you hire quits or is fired within the first few months, you probably won't have to pay a second fee for a replacement nanny. Be sure and check with the agency.

An agency can serve a useful role as a go-between if problems arise between you and the nanny. It can also help you make the relationship businesslike and professional.

To find a reputable agency, talk to friends and check with the Better Business Bureau. The agency should be in business for a number of years and have thorough screening procedures. Ask for written information on the agency's procedures. What standards or qualifications do they look for? How many successful placements have they made in the past? How many people do they interview before sending you a suitable candidate? Ask for references from satisfied clients.

You can also find nannies through community colleges that offer courses in child care. Canadian Mothercraft trains child care workers. The early childhood education programs at community colleges are an additional resource. In Montreal, the Canadian College for Nannies trains and places their students.

Place your own newspaper ad for a nanny and save on agency fees. State your requirements briefly: live-in or live-out, hours, your location, whether or not you expect light housekeeping, number of children and their ages, experience, and references required. The classifieds win a quicker response than ads you post in the neighbourhood.

Screen telephone callers carefully. Repeat your basic requirements, then ask the caller about her age and health, her experience and qualifications. How long was she at her last job? Why did she leave? Request references. If you are satisfied with her replies, set up an interview time and ask her to bring along her social insurance number and her visa or landed immigrant papers if she is not Canadian-born.

That said, many child care workers in this country are here illegally and are hired illegally by working parents. They are usually paid less but there are risks attached to this arrangement. You can be fined for hiring an illegal immigrant. The person you hire will not have had the medical examination mandatory before entering the country, thus posing a health risk to your child. Her expenses will not be tax deductible, since she has no social insurance number. And you may find yourself tangled up with awkward immigration problems if she needs help later with the immigration authorities.

A work permit issued to a foreign nanny is only valid while she works for the family who obtained the permit for her. So if a nanny tells you she has a work permit, she will be an illegal immigrant unless you arranged the permit for her originally or obtain a new one for her. You must also renew your nanny's work permit after one year to protect her from being deported.

Whether or not you use ads or an agency, if the nanny you want to hire is foreign and hasn't yet moved to Canada you must fill out a form at your local Canada Employment Centre—form EMP2151, confirmation of employment. Once the form is validated, send a copy to the foreign nanny, who then must present it to a Canadian visa office in her own country. You must also sign a contract outlining the nanny's duties, hours and wages.

Once you have found a nanny you like, you have hired her and the household is running smoothly, do everything you can to keep her happy with the job—good help is hard to find. Nannies can pick and choose their employers so an unhappy one will have no trouble finding a new family.

Make an effort to communicate. Ask her to tell you about the day's activities and encourage her relationship with your child. Let her know what you like and what you don't like about her work. She needs feedback, like any other employee. It's easy for you to start taking her role for granted, but when you remind her of how important her contribution is to all of you, you will help her to feel comfortable with you and your child and to enjoy her place in your family. Don't forget that the foreign nanny is also trying to adjust to a new country, perhaps a new language. Do whatever you can do to make the adjustment easier.

Establishing a solid, close relationship with your nanny is

essential when problems do crop up. Small irritations need to be resolved immediately, in a straightforward fashion. This is far easier when the atmosphere is warm, open, and friendly. Otherwise, minor annoyances quickly blossom into major ones.

One common complaint from nannies concerns working parents who take advantage of their live-in babysitters. Chris, 23, is a British-trained nanny who emigrated to Canada and was placed with a suburban working couple. Chris cared for the pair's two children, three and seven years old. "Both parents worked long hours and it became clear very quickly that they were having marital problems. They argued all the time. That was bad enough, but after a while each parent began staying out later and later. I was left to look after the children from seven in the morning often till ten or eleven at night."

Chris stuck it out for a year, finishing her contract, but finally decided to leave. "The worst part about going was leaving the children. I had grown so attached to them and I knew that they would just be passed to another nanny."

Outline the nanny's duties before she starts working for you, defining her hours clearly. Keep to the agreed responsibilities, to protect both of you. (You can obtain guidelines for contracts from Canada Employment centres.)

Many a mother offers "frills," like lending her nanny the car, allowing her extra time, or giving her the occasional small gift.

Eve, 35, is careful to pay generous overtime rates to her Mexican nanny, Aracelli, when she and her husband arrive home late. They also pay half of her medical insurance coverage. "Last summer we took her on holiday with us to a cottage we rented and *forced* her to take it easy! We consider her a member of our family."

Fair treatment is the best approach. Treat your nanny the way you prefer to be treated in your own job. Review her salary regularly and keep the arrangement businesslike without making it impersonal.

OUTLINING THE NANNY'S DUTIES:

Dear Gloria:

I would like to confirm the points of our discussions and the terms of your employment as a nanny, to start on April 15, 1989.

HOURS:

We have agreed that you will care for Lindsay in my home five days per week. Although variable, your hours will be approximately 8:30 a.m. to 5 p.m., Monday to Friday. In addition, you may be asked to work Thursday evenings. Should there be any variation in the hours, I will try to provide as much advance notice as possible.

In the event of your illness or absence, you will notify me as soon as possible. Similarly, if I am ill or not in need of your services, I will notify you as soon as possible. In either event, there will be no remuneration.

We have agreed in advance that you will not work from June 10 to 28, as you will be on vacation. I will be responsible for providing substitute day care.

We have agreed that until June 10, you will be on probation.

RESPONSIBILITIES:

Your responsibility will be to meet Lindsay's physical needs during the day, including feeding, diaper changes and cleanup, naps, and comforting. Playtime will include daily outdoor activity when possible, and will provide learning-related activities for her. Any television viewing will be only as agreed upon by myself.

In addition to taking care of Lindsay, you will be responsible for Lindsay's laundry, maintaining her room, as well as cleaning up after meals and playtime. We have also discussed other assistance such as household laundry, start-

Outlining the Nanny's Duties, cont'd:

ing dinner, or minor shopping as agreed to from time to time.

In the event of any emergency, I have provided phone numbers and medical numbers should these be required. If you have any major concern, you will contact me or my husband at our offices.

FEES:

I have agreed to pay you $5.00 per hour for 44 hours per week. These rates will be reviewed in December, 1989. Salary will be paid by cheque every other Friday. I will be responsible for remitting CPP, UIC, and income taxes. You will be paid 4 percent per annum salary for vacation pay.

In the event that it is necessary to terminate your employment, either party agrees to provide a minimum of two weeks' notice.

I look forward to working with you starting on April 15.

Yours very truly,

NURSERY SCHOOLS

Nurseries generally offer half-day programs, which make them impractical for a working parent. They also rarely accept children under the age of two and the children must usually be toilet trained. But once your child reaches that age, you may find a nursery an attractive option. And there are nurseries that offer extended-hours care. Some working parents combine a nursery program with private care. For the part-time working parent, they can be ideal. And non-working parents often like their children to take advantage of the opportunity nurseries offer for socializing and learning.

Anne enrolled her four-year-old daughter Catherine in a nursery school when Catherine was two-and-a-half. Anne was not working outside the home then but she felt that both she and Catherine could benefit from the nursery school's program.

"I was going a little stir-crazy at home. I needed to have time away from Catherine and she needed to be around other kids. From the first day, she loved nursery school and couldn't wait to get there every morning. When I decided later to start working part-time again, Catherine was already beautifully settled into the school and the transition was painless."

Nursery schools are often based on a specific educational philosophy. Montessori schools, for instance, follow Maria Montessori's teaching methods and stress a child's independence and creative potential. This is probably the most famous and popular brand of nursery school in North America.

ALTERNATIVES

Part-time work is a compromise that lets some parents enjoy the best of both worlds. They have more time with their children, yet they stay active in their careers.

Financially, it is usually a break-even proposition. Child care costs can cancel out the part-time worker's salary. But if a family can afford it, the part-time option can bring a comfortable balance of work, home, and family.

"I wasn't willing to work full-time after Cathy was born," says Anne, 35, a Toronto nurse. "So I took a part-time nursing position at a downtown hospital, working evenings two or three nights a week. A babysitter came to the house to look after Cathy and when my husband got home after work he would take over. Later, when Cathy was two-and-a-half, we enrolled her in nursery school.

"In these last few years I've been able to keep up my professional contacts and stay in touch with what's going on in the field. It's true that you don't feel quite as involved when you're only at the job a few days a week, but being able to keep my home life on track and spend more time with my daughter has made up for that."

Making child care arrangements can be easier when you don't need full-time care. A neighbourhood babysitter, for instance, may prefer the shorter hours.

Job sharing is one form of part-time work. One job is shared between two employees — occasionally husband and wife. Job sharing is still rare in both Canada and the U.S. Employers are usually small firms and teaching is the field that has adopted this alternative most.

A few mothers have managed to take their children to work with them. They are, however, a privileged minority. And they all give credit to open-minded employers (if they aren't self-employed) and tolerant colleagues.

Others who run their own businesses make room for baby too. But in general this is an option limited to women with power.

Working at home can be the answer when you want to stay on the home front but maintain a career. Unfortunately, the number of professions that lend themselves to a home-office setting is limited. Currently most home-based working parents run their own businesses. If working from home is an option for you, you will need to make preparations. A separate office is essential, where you can escape from household distractions. Despite being at home, you will need child care if you plan to work full-time. And make sure that you have the right temperament for at-home work. Strong self-discipline is necessary and if you count on office companionship you may find working at home too solitary. Those who make it work, however, love the freedom, the flexible hours, and their availability to their children.

Eve, a freelance writer, has a one-year-old daughter, Thalia.

Eve had already worked at home for some years before Thalia's birth. When her daughter arrived, Eve hired a nanny who arrives each morning to care for her child until late afternoon.

"My office is next door to the nursery so I'm well aware of what Thalia's doing during the day. I can run in to see her anytime. For me, this is the best possible arrangement. If you're working full-time outside the home, you have a sense of missing out on your child's life. This way I see her as often as a full-time stay-at-home mother but I'm relieved of the drudgery. I don't feel left out where my daughter is concerned and I'm still working."

EMERGENCY CHILD CARE

It's the working mother's nightmare — a call from your baby-sitter at 7 a.m. saying she can't look after your child today. Or your nanny suddenly quits without notice. When you're expected at the office, where do you find emergency care? Maybe a friend, a neighbour, or a relative will rescue you. (It's wise to keep a list of emergency back-up people.) But if not, you may be able to find substitute care through an emergency care service.

These agencies supply temporary caregivers who work in their own homes, come to yours, or provide group care. In Vancouver, a service called Granny Y's Short-Term and Emergency Child Care operates a downtown group centre. The centre cares for up to twenty children and charges an hourly fee.

Toronto's Stop Gap Family Care has a network of people who accept children into their homes temporarily. And Family Day Care in Toronto has a temporary child care service that sends sitters to your home for short periods.

What if your infant is sick? Mothers often complain that they can't afford to get sick themselves; they have to hoard their sick days for when the children are ill. Day care centres don't accept sick children and often babysitters don't either. If you can't take time off work, you may be able to find help through a private home-care agency. The agency will send a temporary caregiver to your home, but it's a costly service — $50 a day or more. In the U.S. a few communities have established centres where sick children can be brought for daily care.

Working-parent absenteeism is expensive for employers, yet to date very few companies are involved in providing emergency-care help for employees with ailing children. A recent Ontario pilot project trained students to help out employees during family emergencies but it failed. Companies were reluctant to add the workers to the payroll.

Some employers are understanding about family responsibilities and the employee is not penalized for missing work. In British Columbia, civil servants even have ten days paid leave to tend to their sick children.

Flexible working hours — or flex-time — are another way around the problem of emergency child care. With flex-time or variable hours, you can build up a bank of extra hours, to draw on as you need them. It also allows you to come in or leave early when you prefer. The Canadian companies using flex-time report that the system is popular with their employees and provides benefits to the employer as well.

But until more employers recognize the needs of employees with children, working parents will continue to rely on potluck and a sympathetic boss.

WHEN TO LOOK FOR NEW DAY CARE

Be alert to signs of trouble in your day care arrangements. If you catch them early you may be able to prevent further problems. If not, at least you'll have time to make new arrangements.

In a home care setting, watch for signals that the caregiver is neglecting her responsibilities. Talking to her daily will indicate potential problems. If you find, for instance, that she isn't observing your infant's schedule, discuss it. Does she find it impractical? Are her reasons acceptable? What does she suggest instead? Keep communication frank, but be prepared to recognize that you may not be able to agree. When your ideas are too different, start looking for a new caregiver.

A caregiver's circumstances can change, too. She may agree to care for more children than she can handle. Personal and family problems may arise. She may begin to suffer from burnout. A caregiver who greets you each evening with a litany of complaints, or is relying suddenly on coffee and cigarettes, may be emotionally exhausted. Make sure you are aware of any changes in personality that might be affecting her care.

If your infant is in group care, you'll need to be just as vigilant for danger signs. Any increase in the staff turnover rate, a change in atmosphere at the centre, or lower standards, should alert you to problems. Discuss your concerns with the centre director.

Young as your child is, he too can be a barometer. Changes in your infant's behaviour can stem from poor care.

If you are concerned about the care your child is receiving and your talks with the caregiver have not put your mind at ease, you may want to make a surprise visit or two to the home or centre.

If the situation is especially unhappy, remove your child immediately and make interim arrangements while you look for permanent care. Otherwise, start your hunt before firing the caregiver or leaving the centre. Give reasonable notice and be honest about why you made your decision. It may help the next parent.

Reports of child abuse have occurred in day care centres and with individual caregivers. If you suspect that abuse is involved in your own day care situation, don't just remove your child. Report your suspicions to the authorities: the police or a child welfare agency. You will be doing other parents and their children an enormous favour.

CHAPTER 13

Playtime

PITY THE FIRSTBORN child. Pampered and poked, indulged and adored, the first child is a parent's sweet obsession. In toy marketing terms the infatuation spells cold hard cash. Parents spend more money on their first child than they do on their next ones — 52 percent more, to be exact.

Birth order isn't the only factor that boosts toy sales, however. The baby boomers in turn have created a baby boomlet, a new generation of toy customers. Baby boomers, well educated, affluent, and consumer-oriented, look for quality products for their offspring. They don't object to paying high prices for the right items. Child's play is serious business now.

Two-career couples are another influence. Working parents often feel guilty about absenting themselves from their children and to ease their guilt they buy plenty of toys, books, records, and other diversions.

Play is the first form of learning and it starts in the very first week of life. Infant development studies indicate that children respond to their environment from birth. Babies know a lot more than we realized. To meet the infant's budding — and newly recognized — needs, there are toys to stimulate her senses, encourage her creativity, and speed her intellectual development. You can buy a brand of mobile that "encourages scanning, focussing, tracking, orienting, visual discrimination, visual recognition and pre-reading movement." You can buy a rattle that "allows your baby to master new skills," the first in a series of "child development toys." You can buy a jumping bear for the carriage that doesn't simply jump, it also assists "a baby's understanding of cause-and-effect relationships."

What the producers of educational aids like these often forget is that toys are primarily for fun. All the scientific claims in the world won't help if a toy isn't simple, exciting, and a pleasure to play with.

But the earnest marketing of educational toys is only one sign of the times. The superbaby syndrome has arrived. Parents push their babies to learn earlier than ever. Eager to increase their babies' intelligence, they take courses or enrol the children themselves. The Better Baby Institute in Philadelphia, for example, offers professional parenting courses, seven days of intensive workshops for about $500 U.S.

With flashcards, parents learn how to teach their babies anything from mathematics to Japanese. At the close of the course, they are presented with "professional parenting certificates." Better Baby Video is a take-home version of the same educational techniques. A chain of Better Baby Stores sells computers, kits, and musical instruments — but no toys.

Meanwhile, Small Bytes Computer School offers programming for toddlers, Suzuki schools teach two-year-olds to play the violin, and infants work out in customized gym classes.

Producing brainy babies, fortunately, is essentially an American mania — so far. The Better Baby schools still haven't moved north and Canadian parents haven't yet adopted the fierce, competitive, over-achieving parenting style of their neighbours to the south.

Canadian parenting classes tend to concentrate on promoting strong parent-child relationships, and on encouraging parents to enjoy their children, trust their parenting skills, and relax. To parents anxious to provide the best of everything, from education to designer wear, being confident of their ability to parent is no small achievement.

Playing with your infant is an important part of parenting, so it's fortunate that it's also delightful. Your baby's first toy is you. She responds to your voice, your touch, your smell, your face. People interest her much more than objects. Her own hand is a source of fascination.

As a support system, there is a rich assortment of toys, music, books, and classes to help parents enhance the learning experience from infancy on. Knowing your baby's personality will be important to your selection.

You can expect to make a few mistakes and be occasionally disappointed. She will reject the thirty-dollar educational toy you bought and instead will pounce on the packaging it came in; the obvious charm of the Gund teddy eludes her but she howls in anguish if she loses her fluorescent orange stuffed raccoon. As one sadder-but-wiser mother reports, "I learned that Jenny wouldn't love every toy we gave her. Sometimes she ignored a toy at first, but if we pulled it out a month or two later she might suddenly become interested."

Another mother's experience with her one-year-old daughter is typical of what other parents discover about their children's quirky tastes in toys. "A basket filled with pine cones always fascinates Thalia. She takes them out and piles them back in, for hours at a time. It's turned out to be a favourite 'toy.' "

TOYS

The best toys are ones that are in tune with a baby's stage of development.

The first year is a year of exploration. The baby needs toys that spark her curiosity, stimulate her senses, and challenge her new skills. Texture, music, colour, shape—all grab her interest. She wants things to see, hear, taste, smell, touch, and bite.

In the second year she is developing better motor and language skills. She also likes imagination games. Toys that encourage large-muscle development and tease her imagination are best.

The following list is a guide to age-appropriate toys.

Birth to 3 Months

mobiles • music boxes • play gyms • rattles • squeaky toys • squeeze toys • mirrors (unbreakable) • soft dolls • soft toys • textured large/small balls • rhyming records • pictures

3 to 6 Months

crib activity centre • crib gyms • bath toys • teething rings • play gyms • puppets • blocks • pictures • musical toys • soft dolls • soft stuffed animals • board books • cloth books • records

6 to 9 Months

rag dolls • shape-sorting toys • suction toys • bath toys • busy boards • records • musical clocks • musical toys • board books • mirrors (unbreakable) • roly-poly toys • containers • nesting toys • lightweight blocks

9 to 12 Months

stacking toys • play telephones • rubber or plastic balls • bath toys • board books • records • plastic picture cards • wind-up toys

12 to 18 Months

ride-on toys • push-and-pull toys • rocking toys • big

stringing beads • hand puppets • bath toys • different-sized balls • pounding toys • tool boxes • climbing equipment

18 to 24 Months

simple puzzles • stuffed animals • stuffed dolls • child-sized play furniture • ride-on toys • art materials • sorting toys • wagons • storybooks • simple games • music-making toys • musical instruments • cuddling toys • indoor slide • indoor play gym

TOY TIPS

Do consider safety. Canadian toys must meet federal safety standards but common sense is still necessary. Watch for sharp edges, breakability, rough finishes, dangerous strings, and cords.

Don't ignore "suggested ages" on toys. Your child may be advanced for her age but the guideline may refer to safety, not just intellectual ability.

Do buy quality, not quantity.

Don't be influenced by heavy toy promotion.

Do comparison-shop. Prices can vary from store to store.

Do take into account your child's personality, interests, and skills.

Do choose toys that encourage interaction between parent and child.

Don't buy toys with easily removable parts. Children can choke on them.

Do look for labels that say "flame-retardant," "flame-resistant."

Do select toys that offer high play value. The best toys are versatile and will continue to appeal to a child as she grows. For example, a cradle gym with bright colours will attract a young infant's hungry eyes. As she gains skills she can touch it and set it jiggling. Later she will grasp its handles or rings.

If it contains a music box, the toy's response will captivate her even more. This type of toy grows along with your baby.

Do inspect secondhand toys. Toxic paint is one hazard in old toys.

Don't buy handmade cloth toys with button eyes or other materials dangerous to an infant.

Do remember that household objects can fascinate your child: kitchen utensils, containers, pots and pans, etc.

Don't buy toys made from thin rigid plastic. They break easily, leaving sharp edges.

Do look for a toy-lending library. You can save money and also preview toys before you buy.

Do choose sturdy toys.

Don't ignore your own reaction to a toy. If a toy's shrill noise sets your teeth on edge immediately, pass it up.

Don't forget about storage problems.

Do be alert to sexism in toys.

Do introduce toys to your child one at a time.

Don't be fooled by an "educational" label. Any toy has educational value if your child enjoys it.

Do buy toys from reputable companies. They are more co-operative about problems, easier to contact.

QUALITY TOYS

Brand names in toys can be an indicator of quality. A toymaker who offers a line of toys that are consistently creative and well made earns a parent's loyalty and, not incidentally, simplifies toy buying.

Along with well-known toy manufacturers, however, there are small cottage industries that produce only a handful of children's toys, but offer superior craftsmanship.

In Canada Fisher-Price is the single largest brand name in toys. (It's second-largest in the U.S.) The bright sturdy Fisher-Price toys are kids' classics. They are passed from one child to the next, beloved and virtually indestructible. Parents talk about Fisher-Price in the reverent tones they save for the things in life that truly matter. "Fisher-Price," breathes one mother. "Oh, I love those toys . . ."

Fisher-Price toys are mass marketed. The range of toys is carefully researched and the company's reputation is excellent. It has now branched out into children's furniture, playwear, and educational software, selling more than $35 million dollars worth of products annually.

The Fisher-Price toys display a healthy dash of whimsy. The Dancing Animals Music Box Mobile, for example, features four friendly-faced animals which wiggle to the strains of Brahms' Lullaby. (The fact that the animals are tilted to allow the infant a full view prompts toy stores to bill the mobile as "educational," a sample of how easy it is to earn the label.) The Fisher-Price line is good, affordable, and of solid value.

Northern Lights is the first Canadian company to develop, manufacture and market new toys and games. It is presenting a unique opportunity to Canadian inventors, who are usually forced to take their inspirations south of the border. Started by a Montreal doctor, Northern Lights' first venture is a high-priced line of plush puppets. The Rigadoons Gang includes seven large-as-life dolls, each complete with its own name, clothing and personality. The creation of Elaine McMartin, a Toronto inventor, the endearing puppets are finding popularity with parents and educators alike.

Other Canadian toymakers include Playmates Toys, which has introduced a line of expensive bilingual talking dolls, and Charan Industries of Montreal, the company behind the talking bear Teddy Ruxpin.

European toymakers produce high-quality toys that are often handsome and clever in concept. They come with an equally high price tag, however. Some parents consider their cost prohibitive. Fischerform, Brio, and Simplex are three brands distributed in Canada. Brio and Simplex specialize in cheerful wooden toys; Fischerform has a collection of "play and learn" products for infants.

Sometimes the investment in a well-made European product is money well spent. Anna, a mother of two, has high praise for a Brio wooden train her son adores. And she and her sister still cherish toys sent to them by European relatives over twenty-five years ago. "Toys like that are beautiful, and they last forever."

Brands can be a useful guide when you shop, but don't buy blindly. Examine a toy critically. When you want a mobile for your baby's crib, for example, check the mobile from below. That's your baby's viewpoint. What will she see? Is there enough imagination in the mobile's design to whet her curiosity? Light mobiles are best; the slightest draft sets them sailing and motion fascinates an infant.

Playskool, an American toymaker, markets Bright Skies, an appealing wall mobile with plastic creatures that flutter with the merest breath. Playskool also makes a charming cloth rattle for the very young infant. The fabric is soft and machine-washable and the rattle, called Wrist Jingles, attaches to a baby's wrist or ankle with velcro.

The Infant Stim-Mobile may be the only mobile that claims

THE TOY REPORT

The Toy Report is an excellent guide for parents choosing toys for their children. Produced by the Canadian Toy Testing Council, the annual guide rates toys by play value. Design, function, durability, packaging, and safety are also tested.

Kids themselves test the toys and the Council doesn't mince words when toys don't measure up. It's even taken the venerable Fisher-Price to task for a few items. Recommended toys for disabled kids are also listed. All age categories are covered.

The book is available at bookstores around Christmastime, for about $5.95. You can also order a copy from the Canadian Toy Testing Council, P.O. Box 6014, Station J, Ottawa, Ontario K2A 1T1.

to quiet babies. Designed by a Denver mother, the mobile is black and white and features geometric designs and faces. "The young infant is not interested in rainbows and hearts," Ruth Wimmer Ferguson says. She based her design on infant development research and her own experience in therapeutic recreation. The mobile can be ordered through Bright Baby Products, P.O. Box 10427, Denver, Colorado, 80210. Cost is approximately $14 U.S.

WHERE TO BUY

Toy supermarket stores are springing up like jack-in-the-boxes around Canada.

Toy City and Toys 'R' Us feature wall-to-wall toys, games, baby furniture, and clothing, and a self-service selling style. Prices are discount-conscious. Toy City is owned by Consumers Distributing Ltd. The chain is rapidly expanding (in Montreal it's called Toyville) and the supermarket approach, with bright decor and special "kiddie" events, seems to be a success. Toys 'R' Us is an American-based company which has branched out into Canada.

Supermarket toy stores offer a wide choice of toys and competitive prices but they can drive children to distraction. The sheer number of toys is overwhelming. It's not unusual in these stores to see a child in tears or a tantrum because she can't have every goodie on the shelf. If you plan to visit one of these toy markets, consider leaving your toddler at home.

Canadian Tire, surprisingly, is the third-largest toy seller in Canada. It sells toys only for three months of the year — from October to Christmas — but its sales volume is very high.

Far removed from the high-pressure sales tactics of the toy retailing giants is the friendly specialty toy store. These stores are mostly independent and carry toys that appeal to the owners as much as the young customers. The best of these shops welcome children warmly, even set play areas aside for them and let them sample the wares. The staff is knowledge-able, sales pressure is non-existent, and the environment allows parent and child to enjoy shopping for just the right toy. The

West Edmonton mall boasts the world's largest toy store. And the Kids Only Market on Vancouver's Granville Island is a west-coast toyland.

Toy lending libraries can be invaluable when you plan to buy toys. Run by libraries or community centres, they lend out toys like books. It's an economical way to pre-test your child's interest before you buy. Some of these libraries also offer drop-in programs for parents and kids. The Canadian Association of Toy Libraries can send you provincial and national listings, so you can locate a nearby toy library. Write to them at 1207-50 Quebec Ave., Toronto, Ontario M6P 4B4.

Check craft shows and museum stores for special, hand-crafted playthings for your child.

Mail order is a way to discover unique toys that you won't find anywhere else. Products like these don't get into large toystore chains.

B.C. Playthings is a Vancouver company with both a mail order business and a retail outlet. Their catalogue is filled with imaginative toys and it's as notable for what it *doesn't* include as for what it does. You won't see sexist toys, violent toys, or even Cabbage Patch dolls in this catalogue. The family-run business puts the emphasis on "participatory play." What you *will* see is a thoughtful collection of wooden trains, climbing equipment, art supplies, construction sets, books, puppets, stuffed animals, records, and musical instruments. You can order a catalogue from B.C. Playthings, 1065 Marine Drive, North Vancouver, British Columbia V7P 1S6.

Hearthsong offers a catalogue of children's playthings you can send for. These are homespun items, all natural and high quality, with the stress on myth and fantasy. You can order a child's art smock or a kit to make a cloth doll, a mahogany lyre, or an old-time wooden flower press. The catalogue features over 150 items and can be ordered from Hearthsong, 2211 Blucher Valley Road, Sebastopol, California 95472.

Mothercare-by-Post is another source of mail order toys you won't find at the local department store. Their selection is small but cheerful. Write to them at Mothercare-by-Post, P.O. Box 145, Watford, England.

Family Pastimes sells a unique line of Canadian games. They are based on co-operative efforts, not competition. You can write for a catalogue to Family Pastimes, Perth, Ontario.

Pineapple industries offers toys suitable for children aged five and up. Their Canadian-made products can be ordered by mail from 95 Grand Avenue, Toronto, Ontario M8Y 2Z1.

F.A.O. Schwarz, the legendary Manhattan toy store with floor after floor of breathtaking toys, publishes a toy catalogue. Write to F.A.O. Schwarz, 150 Lackawanna Avenue, Parsipanny N.J.

TOY STORAGE IDEAS

low, open shelves • bins on wheels • toy chests • wicker baskets, painted or natural • stackable bins • ceiling hammock • fabric shoe-holders • orange crates

Stuffed animals can be hung on the walls of the nursery. Attach strips of velcro and the animals will stick to it.

Check toy chest lids. If they slam down, they are hazardous. Remove the lid, cushion the edges with foam or install a "lid support" that lets the lid close gradually. Make sure a child who climbs into the chest can't suffocate.

Silverware trays are perfect for paints, jars, brushes.

Kitchen containers with lids can be recycled to store blocks, play figures, or small toys.

Keep a basket in each room of the house to speed toy clean-ups.

BOOKS

Babies are never too young to enjoy books. You can start reading books to your newborn, who will love being held and spoken to. The bright images on the page will intrigue her and the story's rhythm soothes.

Babylit is a growing movement. Libraries offer story programs for babies and Canadian publishers have joined the trend with new lines of "books for babies."

The library programs are open to infants as young as three months. They combine music and activities with lively readings of children's favourite stories. Teaching young children to read is not the objective. The goal is to establish an affection for books—and libraries—that will continue throughout a child's life.

Another way to awaken an interest in stories in even the tiniest child is to attend a storytelling session. Storytelling is an art form and you can find these performers in cities across Canada. Their gatherings, usually open to the public, feature lively, imaginative presentations of tales that are made up on the spot or told anew. Legends, fairy tales, folk tales, and modern-day yarns all make an appearance. Children are spellbound and infants delight in the magic. Check your local library for a storytellers' ad or refer to a city magazine.

You can jazz up your own story sessions with your baby. Choose brightly illustrated books and leaf through the pages slowly. Encourage your infant to focus on the pictures. Use your performing skills and ham it up—make faces, try on different voices, add extra rhythm to the story's words. Noise, action, and colour are essential to your infant. Make the experience entertaining and reading will become a daily ritual.

Try playing "talking book" tapes for your child, too. Robert Munsch, the Canadian children's author and storyteller, has a collection of his stories on cassette: *Munsch Favourite Stories* and *Mermel, Mermel, Munsch*. Sample a few authors on tape. The tapes are also excellent for car travel.

Board and cloth books are baby's first books. Board books are tough and sturdy, with stiff plastic-coated pages that stand up to a little one's abuse. They are child-sized and the cardboard construction makes them easy to handle.

Cloth books offer texture but parents complain that children find them awkward. Pages are hard to turn and they don't like to lie flat. More often than not, cloth books end up in a corner looking like limp dishrags.

BAABEE books aren't really books, but accordion-folded pictures. Montreal author/artist Dayal Kaur Khalsa based the series on infant-development research. The first four feature bright, stimulating symbols and invite direct parent-child play. The eight books that follow in the series have a conventional book format. The books also include suggestions for games. You can order BAABEE books from University of Toronto Press, 5201 Dufferin Street, Downsview, Ontario, M3H 5T8.

Tot-books is a Canadian line of board books for babies, published by James Lorimer. They are available in boxed sets in both French and English. Titles include *I Love My Babysitter*, *Don't Cut My Hair*, and *Little Bear Can't Sleep*. The storylines take a didactic bent, as indicated in another title in the series, *Peepee in the Potty*.

Dick Bruna and Helen Oxenbury are two pioneer authors of baby books. They remain favourites with parents and children. The Dick Bruna series is a crisp collection of simple, primary-colour images that children love. Helen Oxenbury, a funny, talented artist/writer, makes each of her books a new plaything for the reader.

There are many other authors who will charm your child. For an excellent guide to baby books, pick up *Babies Need Books*, by Dorothy Butler (Pelican). Another highly readable reference book is Michele Landsberg's *Parent's Guide to Children's Books*, published by Penguin.

The following is a selected list of books that come highly recommended. They appeal to both infants and toddlers.

Pat the Bunny, by Dorothy Kunhardt (Golden Press)
A classic, a touch-and-feel book that lets a child take an active part in the story.

Max's New Suit, by Rosemary Wells (Fitzhenry and Whiteside)
This author is always outstanding and this book is just one in a series about Max the intrepid rabbit.

Friends, by Helen Oxenbury (Methuen)
The first in the Oxenbury series that also includes *Playing*, *Dressing*, *Working*, and *Family*.

Goodnight Moon, by Margaret Wise Brown (Harper and Row)
Soothing and nearly lyrical, perfect at bedtime. The illustrations reveal new surprises at every reading.

The Runaway Bunny, by Margaret Wise Brown (Harper and Row)
Another thoughtful book by the same author.

B is for Bear, by Dick Bruna (Methuen)
One in a series of board books by the popular Dutchman. *I Can Count* is another Bruna book for babies.

Whose Mouse are You?, by Robert Kraus (Macmillan)
Warm, comical, illustrated poem about a hapless mouse whose family goes missing. To a child, it's an engaging tale of woe.

Tink Tonk, by Mercer Mayer (Bantam)
This series of board books about a robot's adventures was created by one of the most popular children's authors in North America.

Sam Who Never Forgets, by Eve Rice (Penguin)
Sam is a zookeeper and the story chronicles his activities with his assortment of animal charges.

Big or Little?, by Kathy Stinson and Robin Baird Lewis (Annick Press)
One in the Toddler Series, published by Canada's Annick Press.

Let's Eat, by Gyo Fujikawa (Zokeisha)
A board book for infants, with striking illustrations.

Teddybears 1 to 10, by Susanna Gretz (Lion Paperbacks)
Ten enchanting teddybears in slapstick action. They reappear in *Teddybears ABC*. Irresistible chanting material.

Mommy, Buy Me a China Doll, by Harve and Margot Zemach (Lion Paperbacks)
A wistful girl begs her mother for a doll and her mother's answer is a lullaby in prose. The language is rich and rhythmical, the story only grows better with age.

Each Peach Pear Plum, by Janet and Allan Ahlberg (Collins)
Favourite nursery rhyme characters hide in handsome illustrations and the young reader searches out every one.

RECORDS

It all started with *Lullabies from the Womb*.

A Japanese obstetrician, Dr. Hajime Murooka, recorded the noises within the womb of an expectant mother. When soft music and the womb sounds were played to crying infants, they grew silent and often slept.

A record was made and parents everywhere tried the doctor's theory, with uneven success. Since then, the Japanese record has been joined by a few others aimed at babies.

The Baby Record is a collection of lullabies, nursery rhymes and play songs. Bob McGrath of Sesame Street and Katharine Smithrim, a Canadian singer and teacher, sing the tunes and encourage parents to play and sing with their babies ("now, as you sing, run your fingers over the baby's tummy and up to his chin . . .").

This record was followed up by *Songs and Games for Toddlers*, recorded by the same pair. Again, the emphasis is on activities for parent and child. Both records are the work of Kids' Records, a Canadian record producer.

Lullabies and Laughter is another baby album, this one by Vancouver singer Pat Carfra. Traditional lullabies are its focus, with play ideas thrown in.

Rocking Horse Dreams is a collection of familiar lullabies. The 30-minute cassette by Susan Trudell is available by mail order. Write to her at Rocking Horse Dreams, 1481 Paisley Road, North Vancouver, B.C. V7R 1C4. *Golden Slumbers* (Caedmon) is a folk lullaby album with Pete Seeger and Oscar Brand. *A Child's Gift of Lullabyes* and *Lullaby Magic* are also popular with parents and babies.

Canadian children's records are doing a thriving business. Their hallmark has been quality, a feature notably absent in American kids' albums. The U.S. has never been too interested in this market, though this is changing as Canadian records start to sell well south of the border too.

You can find a wide choice in Canadian children's music. The country has produced a group of children's performers whose records have been runaway bestsellers: Sharon, Lois, and Bram, Raffi, Sandra Beech and others. Even the youngest child enjoys music by these performers.

Record stores carry selections of children's music and children's bookstores often include a section for their records.

CLASSES FOR INFANTS

Programs geared to infants are growing in popularity. Some emphasize physical activity, others musical skills, still others concentrate on parent-infant relationships.

If you're looking for a program for your child, check with your public library. They often offer story sessions and creative play programs. They can also help you find other resources in the community. You can contact school boards, parks and recreation departments, community centres and the YM/YWCA about their programs, too. Private instructors may advertise in local newspapers and magazines. Ask other parents to recommend programs too.

Before you sign up for any courses, observe a class. The emphasis should be on fun. In a good program, parents and babies are obviously enjoying themselves. The session is filled with play activities and the instructor encourages parent and child to touch each other, communicate and make contact with other parents and children. Avoid courses with strict regimens, demanding instructors or formal programs. You will want these classes to be an opportunity to spend time with your child. They should be fun, not work.

Few child care experts believe that formal exercise is necessary for an infant. The natural kicking and waving that your infant enjoys provides enough physical activity to keep her fit. So watch out for exaggerated claims from instructors about the benefits of baby workouts.

Kinder Gym is a parent-child program available in many communities. Parents and children spend an hour playing games, singing songs and rhymes and enjoying physical activity.

Gymboree is an American import, a sophisticated program of noncompetitive activities, songs and games. Parents accompany their children to the weekly classes, which are 45 minutes in length. Gymboree applies child development research to its sessions and the goal is to help tots develop self-esteem, sensory-motor abilities and social skills. Despite the rhetoric, children seem to love the classes. They feature child-sized jungle gyms, fancy bubbles and other delights. Vancouver, Kitchener and Toronto have Gymboree centres and the list continues to grow.

Playful Parenting is another U.S.-based franchise that has entered Canada. The programs are comparable to Gymboree's and have started up in a number of Canadian cities.

Swimming classes for infants do exist, but you may need to search. Many organized swimming programs are not open to children under two. Check your community centres or local YMCA or contact private instructors.

Parent-and-infant-stimulation courses use exercises, play, and song to stimulate infants and help parents discover their learning potential. Parents find such courses a valuable way to understand their babies' stages in development.

The Institute of Child Study in Toronto sponsors the Infant-Parent Learning Program. Classes are informal but practical and educational too. One mother who attended the course with her son for nearly a year was well satisfied. "It was a wonderful place. You could use it as a support group or as a play experience for parent and child." Courses like this may be offered by schools, hospitals, or community centres.

You can also investigate baby massage. At the Canadian Institute of Baby Massage in Toronto parents and child care workers learn techniques that help them comfort and communicate with babies. Instructors trained in the techniques are located across Canada. You can also rent or buy video-tapes illustrating the methods. Contact the Sutherland-Chan School and Teaching Clinic, P.O. Box 354, Station S, Toronto, Ontario M5M 4M9.

Listen, Like, Learn is a music-teaching method developed by Ottawa's Barbara Cass-Beggs. The Cass-Beggs system is taught by a number of Canadian music teachers, some of whom accept children as young as six months. The courses focus on rhythm, melody, and movement. The Young Children's Creative Music and Movement classes in Toronto follow the Cass-Beggs method: "Musical Beginnings" and "Dance Beginnings" are open to babies of six months.

Other music courses for young children are available but most are open to the two-year-old and older.

EXERCISES YOU CAN DO WITH YOUR BABY

Try to have a daily exercise session with your baby. Make it brief and happy, no longer than 10 to 15 minutes.

Massage

Age: newborn and up

1. Place your baby on her back on a soft surface.

2. Pat one shoulder, then gently massage the arm, from her shoulder to her hand.
3. When she opens her hand, help her to stroke her body and face, then yours.
4. Follow the same technique with her other arm and shoulder.

Arm Stretch

Age: 3 months and up

1. Sit cross-legged on the floor, baby in lap.
2. Take your baby's arms and gently stretch them out, parallel to the floor and shoulder height.
3. Bring her arms back across her chest.
4. Repeat the exercise.

Bicycle

Age: 3 months

1. Place the baby on her back. Hold both of her legs.
2. Gently rotate her legs in a bicycling motion. Make six rotations.
3. Repeat in the opposite direction, again six times.

Legwork

Age: 4 months

1. Sit the baby on your lap, facing you.
2. Let her push against your stomach with both legs.
3. Hold out the index finger on each of your hands.
4. When she grasps both, pull her hands gently so she gradually pulls herself upright.
5. Sit her down and repeat the exercise.

CHAPTER 14

Holidays

"BEFORE THE BABY, we travelled all the time. We went south for a week or two every winter, we took a summer holiday, we'd go to Vermont for a few days to ski. We'd take a weekend and visit a different city, sightsee, go to galleries. Now, of course, it's different . . ."

Is travel possible after a baby? Or is it fated to become a fond memory, part of the carefree, childless lifestyle you left behind — along with sleeping in on Sundays, reading entire books, and taking five minutes to leave the house, not thirty.

Many parents don't put their holiday habits on hold when a baby arrives. If they are older, travelling may be a way of life. If both parents work, vacations are a chance to spend time together with their baby. And if they like to travel, their new role as parents isn't enough to keep them at home. Infants travel free (or nearly free) on airlines and trains and accommodation is also gratis for them, so parents take advantage of these arrangements while they can.

Without a doubt, though, travelling with a child is very different from travelling without one. It's not for every family. Gone are the marathon museum hops, the spur-of-the-moment getaway weekends, the romantic evenings alone. Babies will change your travel experience. You'll need to plan your trips carefully.

224

Bringing a baby along can complicate travelling, but it can also make the trip a delight. Parents who recommend it mention the pleasures of introducing a wide-eyed, gleeful baby to sand, sea, and sun. They talk about friendly encounters with baby-loving co-travellers. They find, to their surprise, that they like to travel at the slower pace a baby imposes.

Of course there are the disaster days. Days when the baby teethes fretfully or howls through a five-hour flight or refuses to sleep despite all your efforts. That's where mental preparation comes in handy. No, this will not be a "real" vacation. No, it will not be the way it used to be pre-baby. But you can still get away from home, enjoy your child, and see the world.

Anna, 32, took a seven-week holiday in Italy with her husband and two children. Simon was six months old, Clara was almost three. They rented a house in Sicily with another family (the rent was especially affordable when it was split between the two families) and spent their days shopping, cooking, and taking daily trips to the beach. On weekends they toured nearby towns and villages.

"We had a fabulous time," says Anna. "The kids didn't cramp our style in the least. On the beach we would rig up a tent for Simon and coat him with sunblock. When we were out walking on the streets people were very good about helping. They would give us a hand climbing onto a bus with the stroller, even help us find a restaurant. We were surprised to see that there were very few families on the streets of Italy and we were a real novelty. We got lots of attention."

Another pair of hardy travellers, Duane and Evelyne, have taken their children along on annual overseas trips since their birth. "We always liked to travel and we had no reason to stop when we had children," explains Evelyne. "My parents travelled with us when we were young so I suppose that was partly why I took it for granted. I never had the idea that when you had kids you stopped travelling."

Their trips have included a Channel crossing when Eric was two weeks old and a U.S. holiday when Alexandra was three weeks. "We couldn't have done it if I hadn't been breastfeeding. In Europe and England breastfeeding is much more accepted than it is here. I've nursed my babies in department stores on Oxford Street in London, even in Hyde Park and Trafalgar Square.

"There have been times when they were cranky but if they cried, they cried and we carried on driving. We had a few awful plane trips, though nothing we couldn't cope with — people were very helpful and the crew always seemed to have everything we needed.

"We didn't carry along a lot of equipment. The children took a few favourite toys and I had a twin umbrella stroller for them. They never became ill and they still travel beautifully.

"We changed diapers on a bench in the British Museum or in a gallery while we looked at paintings. We spent a lot of time in parks and usually chose middle-of-the-road restaurants, not fancy but not fast-food either.

"Having children didn't change our travel habit. I do remember, though, one desperate night on holiday when Sacha lost her pacifier. We had to search all evening until we found a drugstore that carried exactly the same type."

The travel industry has been slow to catch on to the new wave of parent travellers. Programs geared to them are hard to find. Whatever your budget or your tastes, however, you can plan a holiday you'll enjoy. And while your child is small, he will be only a modest expense.

WHERE TO GO

For the affluent: a three-week cruise on the luxury liner the Queen Elizabeth II, with sumptuous quarters, *haute cuisine*, spa facilities and all-day nursery care for the baby. All of this, and for not much more than the price of a new compact car.

Club Med offers vacation resorts in locations like Mexico,

France, the Caribbean, and Egypt. Their packages are all-inclusive, with food, accommodation, and a wide choice of sports and recreation facilities. The Club has successfully shed its formerly racy reputation. Some of its resorts are now family-oriented and provide full infant-care programs. The Baby Club is open to toddlers from four months to two years and has a fully equipped nursery. The Mini Club is available for the older child and the program runs from 9 a.m. to 9 p.m. All clubs are staffed by experienced personnel. Be warned, the price tag is high. But then, extravagance does seem to go hand-in-hand with hedonism.

Cruises are a trouble-free choice for a holiday with baby, if you can afford it. You can relax by the pool, dine on gourmet meals and enjoy a variety of sports. Laundry facilities, nearby medical help, and an on-board babysitter for evenings out are services especially convenient for the parent.

What about a villa vacation? You can rent a villa in nearly any country and enjoy the conveniences of home — a kitchen, a backyard, perhaps even a beach or ski slope out back — frequently at a price lower than a hotel room. Sometimes the villa comes complete with maid service. Sharing with another family will cut down the cost dramatically.

Holidays like these may be beyond your budget. But cheaper choices like cottages, lodges, backpacking, or camping are still fun with a baby in tow.

One of the best allies the adventurous parent can have when planning a family vacation is a good travel agent. Choose one with kids of his/her own and a sympathetic attitude. Ask your travel agent to check out baby facilities at the location you are interested in.

In response to the demand for family vacations, a few specialized travel services have sprung up. Travel with Your Children (TWYCH) is a resource information centre that searches out holidays appropriate for families. It's not a travel agency, but an excellent source of travel information. Their monthly newsletter, *Family Travel Times*, features cities, resorts, hotels, cruise lines and airlines that welcome children and provide special facilities for them. You can read up on villa vacations, ski holidays, and how to rent a home or apartment in another country. You can find out which ski resort takes infants in diapers into its nursery, and which ships are child-friendly. The newsletter focusses on family vacations in the United States, the Caribbean and Europe, but some range as far afield as Nepal. (A company called Above the Clouds Trekking offers a family trek each December, with porters to carry gear or children.) A sample issue of *Family Travel Times* is $1. Subscriptions are $28 per year for twelve issues. Write to them at 80 Eighth Avenue, New York, New York, 10011 (phone 212-206-0688). TWYCH also produces other publications such as *Cruising with Children* and *Skiing with Children*. A brochure is available from them outlining their publications and services.

Familyworld Tours, in California, offers planned, escorted, international tours in which an adult *must* be accompanied by a child. Trips are available for children from four months of age. Send a self-addressed stamped envelope for a trip-planning kit and questionnaire. The address: 16000 Ventura Boulevard, Suite 200, Encino, California 91436.

If you're interested in an overseas trip, ask your travel agent to recommend the best hotels for babies. Or write to the tourist bureau in the country you're visiting. Europe is filled with dozens of hotels catering to families. In Switzerland, for example, twenty-two hotels belong to an association called the Happy Family Swiss Hotels. The name may seem overly optimistic by the time you stagger in *en famille*, but the hotels are a definite find. They provide babysitting services, cribs, cooking facilities for making baby food, and high chairs in the restaurant.

There aren't many countries closed to travel with babies. Avoid countries where the water supply is poor. Exotic locales are safer when the baby has reached six months of age and has completed the necessary vaccinations. (A breastfed baby is a little safer from the risk of infection.) Check with your doctor for advice on immunization shots and specific concerns. Ask about anti-diarrhea medicine, antibiotics, and Pedialyte. This last is a formula that replaces fluids lost when diarrhea occurs. All are prescription drugs and should only be given on a doctor's recommendation.

Planning is essential for trips such as these. You need to find out as much information as you can before you go. Ask the tourist bureau for detailed information about the accommodation available. If your baby is formula fed, ask about the availability of formula in the country you are visiting. Find out how close shopping facilities are, for food and supplies. Disposable diapers are sold nearly everywhere, but check anyway. Also inquire about local babysitters. Travel bureaus sometimes keep lists of local sitters. Their references may not have been checked, however, so ask around among other parents in case they can recommend people at your destination.

If you are renting a car, arrange a car seat. They are always available, but on a first-come, first-served basis. Reserve ahead of time. Even with reservations, there is no guarantee you'll get it.

You may be charged for the car seat, though some companies offer them free. If the charge is high, it may be more economical to buy a car seat in the country where you're travelling.

Make sure you arrange travel documents for the new traveller. You can list your baby on your own passport free of charge. Present the baby's birth certificate at the passport office and complete an application. You can also apply for a separate passport for him, which requires a passport photo and costs the same as your own passport. Medical insurance is another necessary chore, and it should cover you *and* the baby.

Most parents find that a single destination is easier with a baby along, but another compromise that works well is to establish a base and travel out from there. What isn't recommended is the if-it's-Tuesday-this-must-be-Belgium syndrome. Cramming a dozen countries into a three-week holiday is exhausting enough for adults. Add a baby and the "holiday" will be an ordeal.

Renting a villa, house, or condominium can solve laundry and feeding problems. They also offer comfort and privacy. Exchange clubs match families and destinations. You can also ask a travel agent, or check the classified ads.

Bed and breakfast accommodation is an inexpensive option. Let the host know you have a child. Some hosts don't accept them; others are delighted to welcome a baby into the house and keep a crib, high chair, and so forth available for families.

You don't have to go far afield to vacation. Bed and breakfast lodgings are available nearly everywhere. A lodge or resort can be a relaxing holiday with even the youngest child, and you may not have to travel far to find one. Even if they don't offer infant-care programs, they include meals and recreational facilities and you can usually hire a babysitter for an occasional evening out.

Monica and her husband John took their daughter Michaela on a trip to the Maritimes when she was five months old. They stayed in a bed-and-breakfast inn, putting Michaela to sleep at night on a mat beside their bed. "We did a lot of beach walking and gentle hiking. She rode in a backpack for the first time and absolutely loved it," says Monica. "It was a great novelty; she could look around everywhere as she went. The drive down was hard, though. She didn't like sitting in the car seat and we had to stop a lot to calm her down. I would nurse her or we'd walk her for a little while."

For Boyd and Debbie, a summer stay at a rustic Muskoka lodge was a peaceful holiday. Their four-month-old son Jonathan could join the daytime nursery program and an evening babysitting service was also available. The lodge was family-oriented, with a variety of supervised activities for the young set. "We had a sense of freedom while we were there," says Boyd. "We didn't use the nursery much but if we felt like a game of tennis, we could play for an hour or so and Jonathan would be well looked after. We spent most of our time with him, taking him into the swimming pool or down to the lake, going for walks in the country. On a few evenings we hired a sitter and saw a local play or enjoyed dinner alone. We went back the following summer too."

A cottage can also provide a summer getaway opportunity. Renting one for a week or more with another family is a way to share child care and enjoy some extra company. (Most parents recommend renting with other parents, since additional little ones help entertain the baby.) The atmosphere is casual and if the sun shines the break will be a success.

Make sure the cottage offers enough amenities to make baby care practical. If you don't like roughing it, you'll be less than thrilled by a two-week holiday spent hand-rinsing baby items and boiling water.

Camping and backpacking are still possible with a baby, if you are enthusiastic and have plenty of patience. Again, planning counts. Choose a location where stores and supplies are accessible and don't expect to keep up the strenuous pace you might have insisted on before the baby's arrival.

Before you try an extended holiday with the baby, take a trial run. A weekend trip, perhaps to understanding relatives, will let you test your baby's travel tolerance — and your own.

Some parents bring along a nanny or a baby-mad young relative who is willing to help out with child care. If your plans include stopovers at friends' homes, try to stay with people who also have children. Their first-hand experience of parenthood will make them more sympathetic to late-night crying spells and your interrupted conversations.

Having a baby doesn't have to keep you housebound. Take enough time to plan ahead. Lower your expectations; unless you opt for a travelling nanny, you will still be looking after the baby, so this won't be a completely carefree vacation. But you can enjoy a change of scene and a special time with your child.

PACKING

Packing for the portable baby is not unlike military strategy. You have to anticipate every possibility and be prepared for it, like a general planning an invasion. Your baby may weigh less than a sack of potatoes, but he needs so many supplies that by comparison an army travels light.

First of all, start making lists. Keep track of everything you'll need and begin organizing, not the day before you leave, but weeks before if possible. Save the list for next trip. Add to or subtract from it when you figure out what works.

Know the climate at your destination. An armful of fuzzy blanket sleepers will be useless in tropical heat but sunhats and sunscreens are essential. For a winter weekend in a northern lodge the sleepers are perfect, along with plenty of woolly sweaters and perhaps a few extra quilts for the crib.

Pack twice as many clothes as the baby needs at home. A laundromat isn't always easy to find and babies seem to run through more clothing when they're away. The last chore you need when you're on holiday is a daily session at the bathroom sink, so pack extra babywear for insurance.

An oversize bib will help the baby's clothes to stay clean. You can buy disposable bibs; one brand name is BIB-AWAY. A package of fifty bibs is available from BIB-AWAY Corp. for $3.49 U.S. plus 75¢ for postage. Write to them at P.O. Box 22802, Beachwood, Ohio 44122. Disposa-Bibs are Australian imports now available in Canadian stores, in packages of ten.

If you're heading to a warm-weather spot, of course, baby's clothing will be lightweight and his wardrobe will be simple. Cotton T-shirts and summer sleepers are a breeze to rinse out if he runs out of clean items.

In general, a lightweight wardrobe is preferable. It takes up less luggage room and will be easier to hand-wash if you run out of clothes and can't find laundry facilities. Choose cotton over corduroy or denim. For a summer hiking or camping holiday, cotton clothing is better than synthetics; it breathes, whereas synthetics retain heat.

Make sure all the clothes you pack for the baby still fit. Try everything on before departure, because he may have grown out of clothing you'd planned to take. And think about layering clothes, so you are ready for sudden weather changes.

Can you buy disposable diapers at your destination? They are available almost everywhere now but in some parts of the world they are an expensive commodity. If you know that the price will be high, consider carrying your own supply. It will be a bulky extra, but you only need to take them one way. Pack them in the corners of suitcases to save space. (You can roll up terrycloth sleepers and tuck them in the corners of soft luggage as another space-saver.)

If Europe's your destination, know your baby's weight in kilos so you can buy the right size of disposable diapers. One kilo is equal to 2.2 pounds, 10 kilos is 22 pounds.

Consider taking along a room intercom. They are handy in hotel rooms or when you're visiting friends.

Sample-size containers of powder, diaper cream and baby wipes are convenient for travel and worth the added expense. Add a roll of plastic sandwich bags to use for wet diapers.

A plastic changing pad is also useful, because diaper-changing facilities may not always be available en route. Snugli makes an all-in-one diaper bag with a vinyl changing pad that is particularly handy if you're in transit.

Be selective about the luggage you bring. A duffle bag or a backpack can hold the baby's gear but keep one lightweight bag as a sort of survival kit for him — and you. A waterproof one is best. In it include:

- a day's supply of disposable diapers
- formula (if he's not breastfed)
- extra bottles
- an extra pacifier
- diapering toiletries

- a change of clothing
- a washcloth
- a receiving blanket
- a few small toys
- changing pad
- 2–3 jars of babyfood
- medication and vitamins
- teething gel if necessary
- a sunhat, sunscreen, and insect repellent, if necessary.

Keep this bag with you. If you're flying, add a few extra changes of clothing. Even if your luggage goes astray, you'll have enough supplies for the baby until your baggage arrives or you buy replacement items.

The breastfed baby is the easiest traveller. Don't wean your baby if you plan to holiday in the near future. You can nurse him just about anywhere and the familiarity of your breast may help to soothe him in a strange environment.

If your baby is formula-fed and you're visiting foreign countries, check on the availability of formula there. The tourist association should know. You can take along enough dry formula with disposable bottles to last the length of your vacation, if necessary. Not all babies happily adjust to a change in formula, so you may want to rely on the type your baby is used to at home or experiment with new brands before you go. Overseas you'll find formula made by Ross Laboratories, Mead Johnson and Wyeth Labs is sold under the same product names, except for Similac, which is called Multival in Germany. Canadian or American embassies will probably carry your brand in their store, in liquid form.

Rely on bottled water in a foreign country, or bring your own. If you want to sterilize water one bottle at a time, take along an electric immersion coil (and a voltage converter if necessary) and boil the water for at least three minutes.

Snugli makes a portable bottle warmer that needs no batteries or electricity, making it especially convenient for travelling families. Bring it along for heating a bottle in a hotel room, on the road or while hiking.

Tiny, portable food grinders are great for the baby who is on the road and eating solids. They are available in sizes small enough to fit into a diaper bag and you can use one to mash fresh fruits and vegetables for homemade baby food.

Don't forget about childproofing equipment. Take along a few electrical outlet covers and make sure any medication you bring is stored safely and has child-resistant caps.

Equipment, of course, has to accompany the travelling baby. This gear can be heavy to carry but invaluable anyway. "We couldn't have made our trip to Europe without the stroller and the backpack," says one veteran mom. If you prefer, you can rent what you need when you arrive. Find out what equipment is available at your destination to save duplicating.

A stroller is first on the list. An umbrella-style collapsible stroller is light and convenient when your hands are full with baby and bags. Since mobility is the priority right now, this type of stroller is the practical choice. Aprica's Newborn Elite stroller is a collapsible model that can be used from birth to the age of three. It has a three-position reclining seat. The MacLaren Deluxe Lie-Back Buggy, made in England, is lighter than the Aprica and costs less but can only be used from five months of age. Perego also makes a line of umbrella strollers.

You may also want to take along a baby carrier. If you don't have one already, buy one a few weeks before you go so that you and baby can break it in. The Snugli Soft Baby Carrier is the front-pack type, while an older baby (five months and up) can sit in a hard-frame back carrier, papoose style. The Gerry Carrier is this kind, lightweight with adjustable straps. The Baby Matey is a fabric carrying pack that sits the baby on your hip and can be easily stored away when you're not using it. (See Chapter 10 for more on buying infant carriers.) Carriers can be indispensable when the terrain isn't suitable for strollers. Cobblestoned streets, sandy beaches, and hilly countryside are a few examples of places where strollers are sidelined.

Bring along a car seat too, if you are renting a car and can't arrange to have it included. (Consider buying a new car seat when you arrive if the rental charge is high.)

Whether you take equipment such as portable cribs, collapsible walkers, or swings and jolly jumpers depends on how much you can handle and their entertainment value to your child. You have to carry all this paraphernalia, so be selective.

Travel beds can be useful as portable cribs (though not in the car, of course). The Snugli Travel Crib is a lightweight travel bed that folds for carrying. One side drops to make diaper-changing easy. The crib has a comfortable foam mattress and the padding is machine washable.

One item you may want to take along is a portable hanging high chair (see also Chapter 4). These chairs clip on to tables and can hold children up to forty pounds (eighteen kilograms) in weight. The folding models are light in weight and cost approximately $25. They are handy in restaurants without high chairs. One popular brand name is the Sassy Seat.

You can also buy a fabric high chair, a sling-style cloth harness that ties around the back of a chair. It can be used in shopping carts or strollers. The Travel Safety Seat converts to a changing pad and is available at Consumers Distributing and other specialty shops.

If you are taking along a toddler or young child, provide a personal back pack for their own survival kits. The pack should be lightweight, with adjustable shoulder straps.

A back pack will leave your child's arms free, yet it is roomy enough to stow a variety of important supplies. Include a snack, some crayons and coloured pencils, a colouring book or two, a story book and drawing paper. Add a travelling toothbrush, a small packet of Kleenex, and a light jacket, as well as a change of underwear.

BY PLANE

When you reserve your seat, choose a flight at a time of day when you usually count on your child to be content. A sunrise flight may be a good choice, since your baby might continue his sleep on board.

Decide whether you want a window seat or an aisle seat. The window seat may entertain the baby, but an aisle seat allows you to avoid clambering over other passengers in your row when you make your diaper-changing dashes. Middle seats are the least desirable.

Be sure to tell the airline that you are travelling with an infant. Children under two are considered "lap children" and travel free on domestic flights (or for 10 percent of your fare in the U.S. for international flights), but they are not assigned a seat. If they have advance notice, however, the airline will try to provide an empty seat next to yours. Slow days and off hours are the most likely times you will bag an extra seat. If you can't reserve seating ahead of time, plan to arrive at the airport early.

Ask the reservation clerk if "skycots" are available: miniature cribs that hook onto the front row. These cots accommodate babies up to twenty pounds (nine kilograms). The cot attaches to the bulkhead and gives you plenty of legroom and extra space for diaper-changing and baby gear. Always request bulkhead seating even if your baby is too big for the bassinet.

If it's a long flight, find out if there are stops or changeovers en route. A non-stop flight is preferable, of course. Flights with extra time between connections are better than those which cut it close, if your child is old enough to benefit from some stretching time during stopover.

Many airports offer nursery facilities. Pearson Airport in Toronto, for instance, has an excellent one. Look for a nursery sign or symbol. The best airport nurseries are large, bright, and filled with toys. They offer nursing areas and vital information, such as which airport stores sell disposable diapers.

Ask which type of plane you'll be flying in. Some planes have fold-down changing tables in their washrooms—Air Canada has these in all its planes, with the exception of the DC-9s. This is a feature you'll appreciate on a long flight.

Can you take your collapsible stroller on board? Some parents find it convenient because treks between plane and luggage pick-up can be long. Airlines generally allow a stroller (often they provide them for use in the airport) but if not, tuck your infant into your baby pack instead.

As a rule, airlines carry babyfood, not formula. They will heat up a bottle for you, however.

SAFE FLYING

Travelling by car, by law you must use an approved car seat for your child. And by plane? Well, here the lack of safety regulations is troubling. You are usually expected to hold your child on your lap during take-off and landing— hardly a safe habit.

In the U.S. you can use a car seat approved by the F.A.A. (Federal Aviation Administration) as long as you have reserved and paid for the child's seat. If the seat is not paid for and an extra seat is available, you can use the car seat. If not, your car seat will be stowed away or checked as baggage.

When in use, the car seat must be secured to the passenger seat at all times, even when your child is not in it. The F.A.A. also recommends placing the car seat in a window seat. You can find out if your car seat is approved by checking the seat for an F.A.A.-approved sticker or by calling the F.A.A. at (202) 426-8374 weekdays. Using a non-approved seat can actually increase the chance of injury.

Canada has adopted similar regulations, but at present the use of car seats in airplanes is optional and airplanes do not have to accept them. The only infant restraint

Safe Flying, cont'd:

acceptable to all Canadian airlines is the rear-facing Love Seat. Check ahead with your travel agent or the airline so that you are aware of their policy on car seat use.

How dangerous is it to hold your child on your lap? Statistics are not readily available to indicate how many children have been injured or killed in airplane mishaps; because children under two fly free, their names do not appear on passenger lists. Two U.S. doctors, however, took up the issue in a pediatrics journal recently. They pointed out that as in automobile travel, chances of a parent being able to hold onto a child under force are slim. An infant could crash into nearby seats or objects and be injured or killed. And if the parent does manage to grip the child, he or she could accidentally crush the child because of the enormous increase in pressure.

The two doctors, Dr. Richard Wilson and Dr. Stephen Sheldon, believe that standard lap belts are not much safer for the two- to four-year old. The belts are designed for adults and are not effective restraints for a small child. (Some airlines, however, do provide special safety belts that snap onto the adult's belt.)

Of course, safety seats will not matter in some airline disasters. But they could reduce, and possibly prevent, the injuries children might otherwise suffer during severe turbulence, on-the-ground collisions, or survivable crashes. Until airlines develop special safety seats for children, however, you will have to rely on your child's car seat or your lap during flights.

Take advantage of the early-boarding privilege for families. It gives you a chance to settle in with the baby and to grab pillows and blankets before the supply runs out. Carry your survival kit aboard the plane, with its provisions of food, formula, diapers, clothing, medication, changing pad, etc.

Prepacked disposable bottles of formula are perfect for travelling and worth the extra money you spend on them. You won't need to wait for formula to cool while you're in flight, or stand in line to wash used bottles and nipples. If you're breastfeeding, wear clothing that allows you to feed the baby easily. You won't be able to nurse in private but if you ask you may be given a secluded spot. A window seat offers more privacy.

During ascent and descent, nurse your baby or have him suck on a bottle. This avoids the pain of changing air pressure in the ears. If your child has a stuffy nose, before you go ask the doctor about nose drops or an oral decongestant. Sucking on a pacifier will also help to relieve the inner-ear pressure and may help later to calm a fretful child. Surprisingly, small children are seldom airsick. It's the cabin pressure changes they usually notice. But even crying may help to equalize the pressure imbalance.

Another preventative measure is to give your child a combination of antihistamine and decongestant (eg. Triprolidine or Actifed) about an hour before departure. If your flight is over eight hours long, give a second dose an hour before landing. This medication helps to keep the nasal passages open and reduces the risk of ear infection, to which babies are especially prone. Ask your doctor about this tactic.

Search out the friendliest flight attendant and ask for help. Find out the most convenient time for warming a bottle or food. During the flight, have a few favourite toys ready to entertain the baby and let him play with novelties like the plane's earphones, plastic spoons, glasses, napkins, the flight magazine, etc.

"We took along a sheepskin mat and laid Simon on it at our feet," says Anna. "He spent the flight happily playing or napping."

When you land, don't try to rush off the plane. Gathering

up baby and baggage will take some time. Sit down and let the other passengers leave first. You can take your time and arrive relaxed.

TRAIN TRAVEL

Travelling by train is a romantic way to see the countryside. Romance and children, however, aren't compatible. Trains aren't designed for babies and young children, so parents rarely choose them for long journeys. A leisurely trip becomes a forbidden pleasure with kids along; the fastest route is also the easiest, on child and adult alike. But children under five do ride free of charge by train.

Trains don't have cribs or high chairs and their limited space makes an extended trip impractical. Short overnight ones can be managed, however, particularly if your baby is small. You can take along a basket for the baby to sleep in, and wedge it securely. A plastic blow-up tub (one brand is the Tubbie) can serve as an emergency bed, or you can use a collapsible travel bed like the Snugli Travel Crib.

A backpack carrier can be a lifesaver on a train trip. You can use it to carry the baby, of course, but if it has a back stand it can also act as a high chair and the compartment behind the sling can hold a few diapers and other vital items. A collapsible stroller is another useful piece of gear, allowing you to navigate narrow aisles.

A first-class ticket guarantees you a compartment together. If you go second-class (or coach), ask the conductor to turn the seats around so you can face one another. You can also ask for bottles to be warmed and commercial babyfood is often available.

Parents sometimes find train travel in Europe or Britain easier than in North America. The trains are better equipped for children and fellow travellers are accustomed to family groups.

CAR TRAVEL

Flexibility is the key when you travel by car with a baby. Buckled up in a car seat, your baby is tightly confined and not every infant accepts the sensation willingly. If your child protests even short jaunts, don't embark on a cross-country journey. But if he tolerates car travel — even enjoys it — include him in your plans.

Make the baby's environment as comfortable as you can. Dress him in layers, so you can avoid major struggles to change his outfit when the temperature drops or climbs. Sunlight can bother a baby's eyes in any season and a hat will help shade him. Or add a light-filtering sheet of plastic to the car window. (Now on the market is a window blind you can attach to the baby's car window. It's made by Alkot.) For extra comfort you can also buy a lambskin car seat cover, which is cool in summer, warm in winter, and absorbs moisture and road vibrations. They can be found locally, or write to Baby Love Products, 4935-50 St., Camrose, Alberta T4V 1P9.

Essentials like disposable diapers, food, and a few changes of clothing should be kept near at hand. Also, keep a collection of toys in the car to amuse the baby. A few new toys are a good idea, to surprise the baby. Now available are toys that attach to the car seat's arm rest. Cassettes are another tried-and-true form of entertainment. Story tapes, nursery rhymes, and songs can calm a restless infant, maybe even lull him to sleep. Turn on the radio or croon a few songs yourself as further distractions. (Cassettes can be found in bookstores, toy shops, or record stores, or by mail. You can also borrow them from the library.)

When the trip is long, move the car seat to another spot occasionally. The rear seat is the safest, but a change of windows can ease his boredom a little.

Schedule regular stops and plan to drive at times when

your child naps. Don't try to cover too many miles each day. It's more important to keep the trip relaxed.

Sometimes a baby refuses to sit back and enjoy the ride, even if he is warm, dry, and fed. If your child reacts like this, don't press on. A wailing infant makes driving too tough. Plan a rest stop. Take a break at the next picnic area or turn into a nearby town. An hour off the road will refresh all of you. Take a stroll, visit the public library, a museum or gallery, a park, a college campus, or a school playground. Any of these places are quiet retreats and will help to restore everyone's equilibrium.

ARRIVAL

Once you arrive, follow a relaxed schedule. A rigid itinerary won't work with a young one in tow. Sightseeing should be kept to a few hours daily and you may prefer to plan it around your child's naptime.

If you are on a warm-weather holiday, your baby will enjoy the beach and the water and the leisure as much as you do. Protect him from the sun, though, with a good sunblock, a hat, and limited exposure. Apply sunscreen every three hours and be especially watchful with a fair-skinned baby. Offer lots to drink, too.

Restaurants pose special problems. Some welcome children, others shudder in horror. You are bound to have a few uncomfortable meals while you are away if your child is occasionally restless and fretful. But you can follow some general guidelines to cut down on these episodes:

- Buffet meals can be a boon to the parent. You don't have to wait for food, there's plenty of activity to camouflage a testy baby—or even distract him—and you can take him for a stroll without missing out on your own meal.
- Sidewalk cafés are another option. Sitting outside is more interesting to your infant and any commotion he makes isn't as disruptive, somehow, in the open air.

- Choose a booth whenever possible, to give you more room for an infant seat.
- Let your child face a window.
- Dine out late, so the baby sleeps while you eat.
- Carry a portable clip-on chair in case the restaurant doesn't have high chairs, or has run out.
- Request a table in an out-of-the-way corner.
- Take turns with your partner in taking your impatient child outside for a breather.
- Take along a few toys to entertain your infant.
- Picnic.
- Call room service.
- Hire a babysitter for evenings when you plan to dine in style. Elegant restaurants and children do not mix.
- Order for your child as soon as you are seated. Children don't like waiting between courses and immediate food can be a good diversionary tactic. Bring along some snacks of your own.

MAGAZINES AND NEWSLETTERS FOR PARENTS

Great Expectations, $6/4 issues and *Today's Parent*, Professional Publishing Associates, 273 Richmond St. W., Suite 200, Toronto, Ontario M5V 1X1. $12/6 issues.

Nurturing, 20 Paperbirch Drive, Don Mills, Ontario M3C 3E7. $15/4 issues.

The Compleat Mother, RR2, Orangeville, Ontario L9W 2Y9. $10/4 issues.

Parent's Information Network, 101-8530-101 St., Edmonton, Alberta T6E 3Z5. $9/6 issues.

Pro Parents Resources, 614 Walmer Road, Saskatoon, Sask. S7L 0E2. $5/5 issues.

Tot Spots, 2330 William Ave., Saskatoon, Sask. S7J 1A8. $15/12 issues.

Kids Toronto, 202-540 Mount Pleasant Road, Toronto, Ontario M4S 2M6. $14.50/12 issues.

Home Base (for stay-at-home mothers), P.O. Box 4104, Station A, Ottawa, Ontario K1S 5B1. $7/4 issues.

United Day Care, a listing of more than 1,000 day care facilities in Toronto. 3000 Bathurst St., #106, Toronto, Ontario M6B 3B4. $5.

Through the Maze, a listing of pregnancy and birth resources in Toronto, 296 Brunswick Ave., Toronto, Ontario M5S 1Y2. $7.75.

Grow Safely, a quarterly publication dealing with safety issues and product recalls. Infant and Toddler Safety Association, 53 Larkspur Cres., Kitchener, Ontario N2M 4W8. $8/4 issues.

Safe Not Sorry, a 32-page booklet highlighting the main causes of children's injuries and how to prevent them. Available from the Canadian Institute of Child Health, 17 York St., #105, Ottawa, Ontario K1N 5S7. $3.

Other useful and free booklets:

Is Your Child Safe? from regional offices of Consumer and Corporate Affairs Canada.

Safety Tips from the Canadian Juvenile Products Manufacturers Association, P.O. Box 294, Kleinburg, Ontario L0J 1C0.

AMERICAN PUBLICATIONS

Parents Magazine, P.O. Box 3055, Harlan, IA 51593. $22/12 issues.

Mothering Magazine, Box 8140, Santa Fe, New Mexico 87504. $18(US)/4 issues.

The Exceptional Parent, (for children with special needs), 605 Commonwealth Ave., Boston, Massachusetts 02215.

Practical Parenting, published by Vicki Lansky, 18326B Minnetonka Blvd., Deephaven, MN 55391. $7/5 issues.

Child, P.O. Box 7612, Teaneck, NJ 07666. $33/12 issues.

Parenting Magazine, 501 Second St., San Francisco, CA 94107. $24/10 issues.

Index

246

Printed in Canada